# Then and Now

## The Life Story
## Of
## Richard R. Ruth

# Introduction

For some time my family has been urging me to write my life's story. I was indeed pleased to know that they would desire to have a hard copy of my life's experiences as a means for their information and also something to pass on to their children.

I have endeavored to recall from memory beginning with my childhood days and including 40 years in the pastorate plus 18 years in missionary ministry for a total of 58 years. So now at the age of 80, I am beginning to write my life's story on this 14th day of February 2016. Since I am writing from memory, I apologize if in my attempts to remember, I fall short.

I endeavored to set as a goal for my life to do my best each day to honor and serve my Saviour, the Lord Jesus Christ with all my heart, soul and mind, and to be a help and encouragement to those I meet along the way.

I found my inspiration to look for ways to help others as I have the opportunity from Mahalia Jackson's song "If I can help somebody along life's way."

*If I can help somebody, as I pass along.*
*If I can cheer somebody, with a word or a song.*
*If I can show somebody, he is traveling wrong.*
*Then my living will not be in vain.*

*If I can do my duty, as all men should.*
*If I can bring that duty to a world that's lost.*
*If I can spread a love message that the Master taught.*
*Then my living will not be in vain.*

*Then my living shall not be in vain.*
*Then my living shall not be in vain.*
*If I can help somebody, as I pass along.*
*Then my living will not be in vain*

Eternity will reveal how well I have met this goal.

# Dedication

This book is dedicated to my wife and children who have faithfully supported and encouraged me especially in those years of ministry that required many evenings away from my family.

# Acknowledgements

I wish to express my appreciation to my dear wife Elaine who was the first to proof read the pages as I wrote them. Next I want to thank Roy and Diane Hertzog for their time and dedication for twice proof reading my story. Last but not least, a special acknowledgement to Alan Russell who so graciously edited and printed this book.

# Table of Contents

# Growing Up

I was born on July 5<sup>th</sup>, 1935 in my new home at 717 Crane Street, Catasauqua, PA. I am not sure what time of day I arrived. I had a brother who was five years older than me. When I was two years old my sister Shirley was born and after another two years, my sister Lois.

Financially we were having it rough. Gasoline for the car was on rations along with other food items. The car windshield had a lettered sticker which allowed you to purchase gas on a certain time schedule. Butter was made from the cream on top of the bottled milk delivered to our door by the milk man. The margarine you bought at the corner store was a white substance with a packet of colored dye that was squeezed into the white substance to give it the color of butter. Rain water was caught and stored in a cistern. A hand pump was used to get the water up from the cistern. This water was used for washing and cleaning, etc. We had an icebox for a refrigerator. The ice man would come to our home several times in the week to deliver blocks of ice. Our bathroom was an old outhouse located several feet from the house. We kept warm in the winter with a pot belly stove in the living room and an old black cast iron stove in the kitchen that would burn either wood or coal. Next to the kitchen stove was a galvanized tub where on Saturday night we took baths. Water was heated on the stove and poured into the tub. The kitchen stove came in handy in the wintertime when we would be outside playing in the snow.

In those days, even though the town had a snowplow the roads were not cleared as they are today. There were very few cars on the streets so sleigh riding was possible almost anywhere. Our favorite place to safely sleigh ride was Walnut Street from American Avenue down the Walnut Street hill toward the waterworks. The town fathers blocked off this street and we could sleigh ride day or night. The other safe place was the three hills at the playground at the foot of Bridge Street next to the swimming pool. When we came home cold and wet we placed our clothing around the old stove in the kitchen, opened the oven door and placed our cold feet on the door.

Our house was a converted barn and quite small. There were two small rooms on the first floor, two small rooms on the second and an attic on the third floor. You came into our house through the kitchen. When we all sat around the dinner table you could not open the icebox or the stove. The second room served as our living room with a large pot belly stove in the corner. Both stoves kept the kitchen and living room cozy.

When I was about five years old my aunt and uncle, Alfred and Francis Clauser, were expecting their first child. The baby was stillborn which devastated Alfred and Francis because not only did they lose the baby but the doctor told them they could never have any children. My brother Bob was really a half-brother. When my mother was in her teens she was taken advantage of by a neighborhood boy and she became pregnant with Bob. My grandfather would not think of putting Bob up for adoption so they agreed to raise him in their home. Bob was ten at the time that Aunt Francis gave birth. Several years earlier my mother married my dad and they began their own family. We now numbered four children in our tiny house. Bob was ten, I was five, Shirley was three and Lois was one year old. Financially we were quite poor and times were hard. Alfred and Francis came to my parents and asked them to consider allowing them to adopt Bob and raise him as their own.

This of course was a very hard decision especially for my mother. After discussing the matter, it was agreed that Bob would go to live with them and become their son. Even though Bob now had the Clauser name, we were still considered brothers.

My father, Raymond Ralph Ruth, was a paperhanger and painter. He worked for someone else during the day and after supper would do work for others hanging wall paper or painting. There were times when he had no regular work and so did odd jobs until fulltime work became available again. My mother, Naomi, worked in a sewing factory and received a meager paycheck. I remember being sent to the A&P store at Second and Bridge Streets on a Saturday to buy whatever chicken parts were on sale. I was to buy as many of the chicken parts as my mother gave me money. So on Sunday we had chicken. On Monday we had some form of chicken. We had the same menu for Tuesday and Wednesday. By the time Thursday came we were out of chicken so we ate potatoes until the weekend when I would once again go to the A&P to buy chicken on sale. We planted a garden for fresh vegetables. Next my Dad built a chicken coop and rabbit hutches. Now we had fresh vegetables in the summer as well as chicken and rabbit for meat. When we would butcher a rabbit, I was the one to take the hide to the tannery, receive money and return home. The tannery smelled awful and I could hardly wait to get the money for the pelts and ride my bicycle back home. My other responsibility was to take my wagon and go to Race and Canal Streets to the granary to purchase feed for the chickens and the rabbits, load my wagon and walk back about one-half mile to my home. When the feed bags were empty my mother would use them to make curtains or pieces of clothing because each bag had a beautiful floral design.

I attended the Second Street School located on the corner of Second and Walnut Streets, about a block and a half from my home. Today the old school has been torn down and a playground is in its place. The Second Street School went from first through sixth grade.

When I was around fourth grade, I began to take piano lessons. My teacher was Mrs. Young. Mrs. Young lived on Third Street only a few blocks from my home. I really didn't want to play the piano and have to practice while my friends were outside playing, but I tried. I was able to conquer using the right hand and reading the notes but when I tried to put the left hand playing the lower notes with my right hand I was a complete failure. This was the demise of my piano playing.

Next I tried the trumpet. I was given a used trumpet and began taking lessons from Mr. Buck Freeman. Mr. Freeman lived across from Gardner's store on Walnut Street. It was only a half block away from home. I liked playing the trumpet and did well at it. When I was in fifth or sixth grade I was invited to play in the Catasauqua High School Band. This also afforded me many opportunities to play taps for funerals of soldiers through the Veterans Association in Catasauqua. This also meant being excused from classes to play taps. I must admit, I looked forward to being excused from school.

Sometime while I was still in the Second Street School my father spoke with some of the neighborhood men to dig a foundation and move our house over on to it. Under our present house was a potato cellar. A potato cellar is simply a large hole dug in the ground under the house for storing potatoes, vegetables and canned goods. Access to the potato cellar was through a door in the kitchen and down a flight of wooden steps. Behind that cellar door hung one of my father's belts. I knew only too well what it was there for. If I got into trouble, which happened too often, I felt the sting of the belt on my bare bottom.

My father staked out a section of the lawn in front of our house to the exact size of the house. The men in our neighborhood came after supper with picks, shovels and wheelbarrows and began digging a foundation. At night my father would string a set of lights so the men could see to dig. The men would usually work till about nine o'clock. Eventually the foundation was dug, cement blocks laid and a cement floor poured. Next my father contacted Joe Beers from Mt. Bethel, PA to bring a crew of men and his equipment to move the house over onto the new foundation. Mr. Beer's crew arrived with large jacks used to jack up the four sides of the house. They had a large truck with a huge winch attached. The men jacked up the house, wrapped a cable around the house and attached it to the winch. They put rollers under the house. My mother filled a glass with water to set on the kitchen table. The men started the winch and the house began to slowly move on the rollers onto the new foundation. Not one drop of water spilled from the glass during the move. Now our lifestyle changed for the better. No more tub baths by the old cast iron stove. No more outhouse. No more cistern water. No more pot belly stove. Now we had gas heat and plenty of hot water. It was now time to make some additions to our house. A new room was built in the front of the house which became our living room. A dormer was built over the living room roof and attached to my parents' bedroom. This allowed some changes for the second floor. There was now room to have a bedroom for my sisters

9

and a small area for a bathroom. It was a very small but functional bathroom. Let me explain how small it was. When you entered the bathroom, you had to squeeze between the tub and the toilet. After going about a foot and a half into the bathroom you were standing in front of the sink. We were so glad that we didn't have to go outside to the outhouse or burn wood or coal, etc. The next construction was to convert the attic into a bedroom for me. I had enough room for a bed, a chest of drawers, a desk and two small closets. We also had a basement with a work bench and a place to hang the tools. At this time in my life I got interested in building model airplanes and railroading. I used my desk to build the airplanes. I put together a ping-pong table to use for building my railroad display. This made my bedroom quite crowded. I had enough room to climb into bed, slightly open my chest of drawers and my closet doors.

I don't remember exactly how old I was but I believe it was about this same time that someone in town gave me a full membership to the Allentown YMCA. In order to get to Allentown, my mother gave me a quarter. That was enough for a round trip trolley ride and five cents left over for a Reese's peanut butter cup.

I enjoyed swimming and was the last man on the relay team swimming freestyle. After taking the trolley for several weeks I decided to keep the quarter and hitchhike to Allentown and back home. Now I had a quarter to spend. When I was finished with swimming practice which consisted of swimming a mile without stopping, I began to walk down Seventh Street to Washington Street to stand there and hitch a ride to Catty. Walking down Seventh Street I came to Liberty Street, turned right onto Liberty and stopped at Yocco's hot dog stand. Now with my quarter I could buy two hot dogs and a Reese's peanut butter cup.

We had a successful year as a swim team. We swam relay and I was the anchor man swimming freestyle. Our record was good enough to finish second in the State finals.

I had lots of spare time on my hands, especially during the summer months. Besides riding my hand-me-down old bike, I would build go-carts from scrap wood my dad had laying around the back of the yard. I made one using an old interior house door. I nailed old wagon wheel axles onto a two by six board for front and rear axles. I drilled a hole in the center of the board which I would use for the front axle assembly. I fastened that board with a bolt, two washers and a nut to allow freedom for steering. I cut out a section of the door and prepared it to use for the braking system. I found an old tire, cut out a section of the tire and nailed it to the end of the section I cut from the door. On the other end of the section I found two large hinges which I fashioned to that section and also onto the door itself. This would serve as my braking system. (Once before when I made a go-cart I forgot to make allowance for a braking system and had to hit a hedge row to stop smashing the front of the cart.) Next I cut some rope and nailed the ends to the board that was bolted to the door. This would serve as a means of steering the cart. I mounted some old wagon wheels onto the front and back axles. Next I built the outline of the cart by using one by two wooden strips. When the outline was finished I covered it with cardboard cutting out a door to get in and some windows. It was ready for a trial run down Walnut Street.

I would also go to the A&P and ask for an empty orange crate and take it home to make a scooter. I would turn the crate upside down and nail a piece of strong board to the bottom. Next I would take one roller skate and separate it into two pieces. I would nail the front piece of the skate to the front of the board and the back piece to the back. After that I would take two short pieces of one by two's and nail them to the top of the orange crate in an inverted V shape to be my handle bars. The scooter was ready to use. I was always trying to build things with the scrap wood my dad had piled in the backyard.

I learned to make a crystal radio set using the toilet paper inner roller, copper bell wire, a set of earphones and a crystal. After removing the outer covering of the bell wire, I would wind the copper wire around the toilet paper roller and fashion the ends to a board where I would attach the ends of the wire to posts for the earphones. One end of the copper wire was scraped clean and used to scratch the surface of the crystal until you picked up the radio station. Another project was to

11

take a six-volt storage battery, bell wire, a flash light bulb and a switch so that attaching them together you would have some light at night.

717 Crane St.
Catasauqua, PA

Mom and Dad on a
stroll

Mom, Dad and me

Grandfather Ruth and
me at 11 months

Mom and me at 1 yr.

Mad they didn't give me
ice cream

Me and my truck

Me and Bob on rocking
horse made by
Grandfather Ruth

14

My mother, brother Bob, me
and sister Shirley

Bob, me, Shirley and Lois

My dad and the rabbits

All dressed up

Me, Shirley & Lois

My dad, me, Shirley & Lois

School days, 2nd St. School, Catasauqua

Me and my go cart

16

Playing my trumpet

# High School

After graduating from the Second Street Elementary School I became a student at Catasauqua High School on Howertown Rd. The High School building was used for Junior High grades seven and eight, and High School grades nine through twelve.

While in Junior High I learned ways to earn spending money. I went door to door collecting old newspapers. I tied them into bundles, loaded them onto my wagon and hauled them to a recycling plant where I would get a few cents per pound. I collected discarded glass soda bottles and could get between two and five cents per bottle. In the summer I mowed lawns, weeded an elderly lady's garden, (which I really hated, but I got paid), and in the winter shoveled snow. I also had a paper route getting up early to deliver my papers. My odd jobs didn't pay much money but at least I had money of my own to spend. When I was old enough to get working papers, I was hired by Mr. Driesback, manager of the A&P at the corner of Bridge and Second Streets. Now I received more money than any of my other odd jobs paid me. When football season came around I quit my A&P job and when the football season was over, Mr. Driesback hired me back. I mostly worked in the produce department but also stocked shelves. When they were busy I packed bags and carried them out to the customer's car.

When I entered ninth grade I continued to play in the band but now I also played in the High School orchestra and sang in the High School chorus. Soon I was promoted to first chair in the school orchestra and lead trumpet in the band. When I entered tenth grade I played football for the Junior Varsity team. Fortunately, I was one of the biggest players on the team and at the end of the J.V. season I was placed on the varsity team. I had the opportunity to play for a few minutes in the Thanksgiving game with Northampton. The coach told me that I would be on the starting lineup next season. However, that did not materialize. The summer between my sophomore and junior year, I received a permission slip that my parents needed to sign giving me permission to begin football training for the upcoming season. About the same time my father rather gruffly told me to take the pile of firewood we had split and pile it in the basement. I responded with a tart remark that he should do it himself. My father asked me to repeat it and I did more emphatically. He didn't say a word but simply walked over to the table where the permission slip lay. He picked it up, stood in front of my face and slowly ripped the permission slip into pieces. I begged for forgiveness and said I was very sorry that I said that, but to no avail. Needless to say, I didn't play football that season.

At this point I should explain the background to my explosive attitude. My father was a quiet man. He never had much to say, in fact he wasn't home much of the time having to work for someone during the day and working for himself after supper. When we sat at the supper table there was not much talking allowed. My father would simply look at you and you needed to figure out what he wanted. Was I chewing too loudly? Did he want the salt and pepper? Did he want you to pass something? On top of this he was not very nice to my mother. This bothered me to the extent that I had lost respect for my father and talked about that with my mother often. Since I was head and shoulders taller than my dad, my mother asked me to promise that I would never do anything to harm my father. I don't believe my father had made a profession to trust the Lord for his salvation at that time of his life. His decision to trust Christ came much later. Several years later on one occasion I had the opportunity to have a heart to heart talk with my dad. We talked about those older difficult days. We cried, embraced and that area of our lives was gone forever.

I did play football in my senior year but did not finish the season. On Halloween night in 1952 while playing East Stroudsburg High School, I suffered a fractured ankle that ended my playing football. When football season came around I had quit the band. How could I play in the band and play football at the same time?

While I played in the High School band I had a friend who played drums and lived on a farm on the outskirts of North Catty. His name was Richard Smith. He invited me to come work with him on the farm. Friday after school I would ride my bike to the farm and do chores with him staying until Saturday after chores when I would ride my bike back home so I could go to church the next day. I learned to help milk the cows, slop the pigs, and grind corn for the chickens, ducks and geese. I would ride behind the tractor on the sickle bar and cut alfalfa. When the alfalfa was dry I helped load the hay bales onto the wagon and later helped stack them into the barn. Down deep inside I longed to have the opportunity to drive the tractor. Once I thought I would have the chance when we were told by Richard's father to take the tractor and wagon, go out to a certain field and pick up rocks. I thought Richard would drive the tractor with the wagon to the field and both of us would go down the field and pick up the rocks. He would probably then ask me to move the tractor to the next spot. That didn't happen. I picked up the rocks and he sat on the tractor and slowly moved from spot to spot.

Catasauqua High School band

YMCA Basketball team

Band uniform, 8th grade

# Football

Catty High Varsity Football team #27

Varsity Football letter 1953

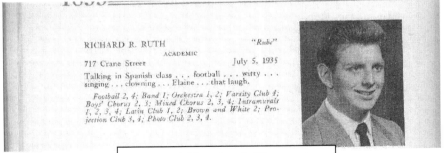

RICHARD R. RUTH                    *"Rube"*
                ACADEMIC
717 Crane Street                    July 5, 1935
Talking in Spanish class . . . football . . . witty . . .
singing . . . clowning . . . Elaine . . . that laugh.
  *Football 2, 4; Band 1; Orchestra 1, 2; Varsity Club 4;
Boys' Chorus 2, 3; Mixed Chorus 2, 3, 4; Intramurals
1, 2, 3, 4; Latin Club 1, 2; Brown and White 2; Pro-
jection Club 3, 4; Photo Club 2, 3, 4.*

1953 Yearbook Picture

22

# Church

In 1949 our family began attending Bethel Mennonite Brethren in Christ Church on North Eighth Street in Allentown, PA. (Several years later the name was changed to Bethel Bible Fellowship Church.) We became regular attenders and I began to play my trumpet in the Sunday school orchestra and occasionally trumpet solos in church. I also became a part of a male quartet as well as singing in the church choir. I began attending Menno Youth group and also sang in their chorus. It wasn't long after attending Bethel Church and especially going to the youth group that I took notice of a very pretty girl by the name of Elaine Metzger. I am sure we spoke to each other while we were in the youth group and also singing in the church choir.

I found some real friends at Bethel: Neil Taylor, Bud Roberts, Dallas Decker and Ken Brobst. These friends were five years my senior and all had driver's licenses. I was only fifteen so my friends would come to pick me up and take me to youth meetings, socials and other get-togethers. That summer I was invited to join Neil, Buddy, and Dallas for a week at Word of Life Camp at Schroon Lake, NY. Neil drove his 1932 Ford and we all piled in. While at the camp we all stayed on the island which was one mile across Schroon Lake from the mainland. I found another friend on the island who was on a swim team in his home town. We challenged each other to swim the lake. After talking about this with our counselors they agreed to allow us to swim the lake providing we took a canoe and another friend and rowed to the mainland. Once there we could dive into the lake and swim back to the island followed by our friends in the canoes. The water was cold but we both managed to reach the island a little exhausted but successful.

Every night Dr. Harry Rimmer spoke in the evening service. He spoke from John 5:24, preaching from a different phrase of that verse for the five nights.

"Verily, verily I say unto you,
He that hears My word

and believes on him that sent Me,
has everlasting life,
and shall not come into condemnation;
but is passed from death unto life."
--John 5:24

God really spoke to my heart. I knew that I had accepted the Lord some years before when I went forward during a church service at St. John's Evangelical Congregational Church on Walnut Street in Catasauqua where we attended at that time. However, I had not grown much spiritually and God was speaking to me about dedicating my life to Him. I didn't commit myself to the Lord at Word of Life Camp but on returning home the following Saturday, I went to Mizpah Grove Camp Meeting service sponsored by the Mennonite Brethren in Christ Church and dedicated my life to the Lord. The date was July 9th, 1949. I will always remember that date.

Bethel Quartet

Bethel Trumpet Trio

My Sweetheart

Getting to know each other

Neil Taylor

Bud Roberts

Kenny Brobst

26

Schroon Lake

Me at Mizpah Grove

# Friends

It was about a year later that Dallas invited me to accompany him on a trip to Montana to visit his aunt and uncle. Dallas's mother was a registered nurse and was caring full-time for Jane Ebby, a mentally challenged girl. Jane's father was the president of the Bethlehem Steel Company. All four of us would make the trip in Dallas's 1946 Fleetline Chevy. This particular model of Chevy was a two-door sedan with a sloping body style. I don't remember the day of the week that we started on our trip but it was in the summer and the weather was a bright sunny day. In order to be as economical as possible we would stop at lunch time to purchase lunchmeat, bread, etc. to make sandwiches. Occasionally we went to a restaurant for the evening meal. I do remember that on several occasions the lunchmeat had turned bad and the tomatoes were rotten because we didn't have a cooler in the car. At night we set up a tent and slept outdoors. One night we couldn't set up the tent because we were in a downpour of rain. We slept in the car. Mrs. Decker and Jane slept sitting up in the back seat, Dallas slept on the front bench seat and I tried to sleep lying as best as I could on the floor boards. It was a miserable, sleepless night to say the least. There were a few nights that we did sleep at a motel.

One of my better moments to remember was our stop at Yellowstone National Park in Wyoming. I remember very clearly when we inquired about sleeping arrangements. We were offered several options. The least expensive were a type of tent/cabin unit. They looked like a tent with four-foot wooden sides covered with a canvas top. The ranger that assigned us a unit suggested that it would be to our benefit to purchase some firewood for the stove because it would get quite cold during the night. After a brief discussion, it was decided that the cost of the wood for one-night stay wasn't in the budget. We enjoyed touring through the park – seeing Old Faithful spout a huge stream of hot steaming water, and experiencing the sulfur springs. After our evening meal, we settled in for a good night's sleep. In the middle of the night I became quite cold. The ranger was absolutely correct. It was really cold. I crawled out of bed and opened my suitcase. I put on all the clothes I could find and went back to bed. I could have been warmer but I did the best I could with the clothes I had in my suitcase.

We eventually arrived at our destination: Billings, Montana. We were welcomed warmly by Dallas's aunt and uncle. I am not sure how long we stayed in Billings, but I do remember being taken to a steakhouse for an evening meal. Outside of the restaurant was a statue of a cowboy waving his arm as if inviting us to come on in. The statue was about fifteen feet high and very lifelike. It was a very enjoyable evening with all of us sitting around a table enjoying our meal. What sticks in my mind about this meal was that it was the first time I ever had steak. Soon it was time to say goodbye and begin our return trip to Allentown.

Saturdays were the days when I would occasionally take the trolley car from Catasauqua to go to Seventh and Hamilton Streets in Allentown. Everybody went to Hamilton Street because that's where the Five and Dime Stores, Leh's and Hess Brothers' department stores all were located. The cost to take the trolley was ten cents one way. You could buy a delicious hoagie at Woolworth's Five and Dime Store for twenty-nine cents. It was on one of those Saturdays when I was in Woolworth's Five and Dime Store that I spied Elaine and her sister Jane. They were sent to Woolworth's by their mother to buy hoagies for the rest of the family. I followed her and her sister around the store and watched them do their shopping.

Shortly thereafter Jack Wyrtzen from Word of Life in Schroon Lake, NY came for a special Sunday afternoon service at Bethel Church. The young people who came to the church services were expected to sit in the front of the church on the piano side of the church. I took my seat with two of my buddies, Buddy Roberts and Kenny Brobst. Behind us sat Elaine, Phyllis Taylor and Gerry Hubner. It was December 3, 1950 and the service began at 3:00 pm. Since the youth group met at 6:00 pm I talked with my buddies and suggested that we ask the three girls to join us after the service and go for ice cream at the Kutztown dairy and then come back for the youth meeting. They agreed and we all piled into Buddy's 1936 Chevy and away we went for ice cream. On the way back to church I asked Elaine if I could walk her home after the evening service. She agreed and after church I walked her to her apartment on North Madison Street. This began our five-year courtship.

All was not smooth because the night I walked her home her mother was not very pleased. She had never met me nor knew anything about my family. So my first plan of action was to get her mother to approve of me. I found out that she liked to play Parcheesi. Then when I would come to see Elaine I would eventually end up playing Parcheesi with her mother. Little by little her attitude toward me was changing. I knew that it was because she began to make me huge Dagwood sandwiches. Next, she knew that I liked orange soda and she began offering me orange soda.

About this same time, I got a job parking and washing cars for Grime's Garage on North Ninth Street in Allentown. The garage was one block south of Hess Brother's Department store and many of the bosses and some clerks would have me park their cars while they would walk to work. I would watch for them at quitting time and have their cars ready for them when they came into the garage. I was fortunate to have this job because I didn't have a driver's license since I was only fifteen years of age at that time. This however didn't seem to matter to Mr. Grime. The only condition he established was to park the cars as close together as you can manage and still get out of the car. If I dented or scratched a fender or the side of the car, I was responsible to pay for it. Needless to say, I had a few scratches or dents and no pay for that week.

Because I was already in Allentown what better chance to see Elaine but to go to their house after work. I was invited to stay for supper. This began a somewhat of a routine. Even on days that I did not park cars I would have supper at my house at 5:00 o'clock, hitchhike to Allentown and be at Elaine's house in time to join with them for another supper. I need to explain that since our meals at my house were quite meager I still was hungry enough to enjoy Myrtle

Metzger's cooking and of course be with Elaine. I had another obstacle to work through. Elaine's twin sisters, Brenda and Beverly who were ten years younger than her, were always around us. In order to have a few minutes to ourselves I had to bribe them each with a quarter.

Myrtle Metzger's
Dagwood Sandwich

Myrtle Metzger cooking

32

# College

In my senior year of High School, it was time to think about college. It was on a Sunday after the morning service that our Pastor, Rev. C. Leslie Miller, said he wanted to talk with me after the evening service that night. When we met he asked me about my plans for my life after graduating from High School. I told him I thought I would attend Berean Bible School, the same school in which Elaine had enrolled as a student. He asked me if I really loved Elaine. My answer was an emphatic yes. He next asked if I was going to enroll in Berean because Elaine was there. He suggested that if I really loved Elaine I should put our love to the test and enroll in another college. Several months later, just before my graduation from High School, a young married couple from Bethel, Bob and Rachel Vogel, who were recent graduates from Bob Jones University in Greenville, South Carolina invited Elaine, me and two others to join them to attend a Bible conference and student open house at Bob Jones University. We enjoyed traveling with them and especially the beautiful campus of Bob Jones University.

Upon returning home and praying for God's guidance for my life I made application to Bob Jones University. A short time later I received their letter of acceptance. I began to make plans for my student life at BJU. I was able to find a good paying job with a brick layer from Bethel Church by the name of Woody Lehr. He had the contract to construct the addition to the Allentown Water works. The next week after graduation I began work as a hod carrier and scaffold builder. A hod is V-shaped wood or metal trough with a long handle used for carrying bricks, cement, etc. on the shoulder. It could be quite heavy carrying the hod full of cement or bricks up a ladder to supply the material to the brick layers. My means of transportation to and from the job site was my newly purchased 1935 Ford that I purchased from a friend at Bethel, Harvey Fritz, for $50.00. The car ran like a top even though it had holes in the floor and very little upholstery on the doors. Someone had removed the original front bench seat and replaced it with two larger bucket seats. They were high enough off the floor boards that a two-gallon oil can was able to fit under the driver's seat. The gas gauge didn't work so I would keep a small tablet and a pencil in the glove compartment to write down the mileage each time I got gas. If I was working I would have money for gas and if I was without a job the two-gallon oil can came in handy. I usually could scrape up fifty cents for gas. I would drive to the gas station but not pull up to the pumps. I was embarrassed to ask for fifty cents worth of gas. I instead would park around the corner from the gas station, remove the oil can from under the driver's seat and walk to the station. It was easier that way to purchase fifty cents worth of gas which usually was exactly two gallons. There were times that Elaine and I wanted to go on a date and stop at the Ritz for a crab cake sandwich for her, an oyster sandwich for me and two CMP sundaes. During those times when my cash was low Elaine graciously paid for the needed gas. She was always generous that way. Elaine was working at a bank at Seventh and Hamilton Streets, and paying her way through Berean Bible School.

My folks let me keep all my pay which was very substantial and apply it to my college tuition. I earned enough that summer to pay for my entire first year at BJU. As the summer came to a close, I realized that my 1935 Ford wouldn't make the long trip to South Carolina. Phil Nuss, Menno Youth choir director and a member of the quartet, had a 1942 Plymouth that he was selling. We negotiated a fair price and I became the owner of a newer car. It soon came time to pack the car and begin the long drive to South Carolina.

My mother bought a large trunk to pack most of my clothes and other incidentals to be shipped to Bob Jones University. The rest that didn't fit into the trunk was packed in the car.

The night that I left for BJU, Elaine and I spent some time with my folks. I later drove her home and at midnight began my trip down south. The car worked fine and I had no problems on the trip. About 2:00 pm the next day I registered my car and registered for my dorm room. My room was on the first floor and my trunk was already in my room. On one wall there were two double-decker bunk beds. On the opposite wall were a desk and a sink with a mirror. The front wall had a large window in the center and on the right side toward the sink were hangers for towels and wash cloths. On both sides of the inside door leading into the room were places to hang clothing. Even though we had four bunk beds in the room I only had two other roommates. One was an ex-service man named Ray and another was a first-year student my age, named Dick Williams. Dick was from Phoenix, Arizona and I am not sure where Ray was from. Dick and I had many things in common; more than I had with Ray. I didn't see much of Ray on a daily basis because he was an upper-class man and had more privileges than Dick or I had. Dick had played football in high school and was offered a scholarship from Arizona State which he turned down to come to BJU. I had received a letter of intent from Moravian College but with my ankle injury I never followed this up. I was taller than Dick but we could wear each other's shirts and jackets.

During the first week of school a lot of time was spent registering, picking up our books and getting the layout of the campus and the many buildings. There was always a group of students outside the dining hall recruiting freshman students to join their society. All student activities revolved around these societies. All sporting events and social events depended on these societies. I was attracted to Chi Delta Theta society because they had a German oom pah pah band. This would be the society I joined. After a few meetings, I was invited to join the band. We played at the Student Assembly on many occasions and during other special events. The band had enough trumpeters so they asked me to play the French horn. One was found in the band room and I started to practice playing this instrument. I neglected to sterilize the mouth piece and I started to break out with sores inside my mouth and down my throat. Simply drinking water was painful. I ended up spending several days in the college hospital until the infection was gone. I also joined the BJU marching band. In the fall of my first year, the city of Greenville sponsored a parade and BJU's band was invited to march in competition with Clemson University's marching band. It took a lot of practice to get the routine down correctly. Bob Jones University had the reputation that whatever they did had to be first approved by the BJU committee and done to perfection. The entire competition was televised and Clemson won first place. The reason BJU came in a very close second was because we did not have uniforms. The girls wore white blouses with blue scarves and blue pleated skirts. The boys wore blue suits, white shirts and maroon ties.

Every Sunday we had a worship service and no one was exempt from attending. The service was very formal and with a lot of dignity. All students were dressed in their finest. The boys were required to wear ties with no exception. Even attending the daily chapel service, they had to wear ties. It became the practice that you would have a bow tie in your pocket so when you went into the chapel you could clip on the bow tie and be legal. I remember on one occasion I left my room without my bow tie. I was wearing my varsity football jacket that had snaps instead of a zipper. As I entered the chapel I remembered I had forgotten my bow tie so I deliberately snapped all the snaps including the snap around my neck. The jacket fit so tight around my neck that it was impossible to tell if I had a tie on or not. If I had been caught I would have received a demerit. Demerits were handed out for breaking the many rules and regulations established by the university. When the demerits added up to five they began to double. After that for any infraction, when they reached one hundred and fifty you were automatically expelled from the university. Fortunately, I only received one demerit that year for leaving an empty soda bottle in my room when I left for class.

Every Sunday afternoon at 4:00 o'clock we had a vespers service. It was usually less formal and many times filled with a series of musical numbers. On one Sunday vespers three members of my society and myself were selected to perform the hymn; "Master, the Tempest Is Raging." The auditorium seated over three thousand students and many individuals from around Greenville. The platform was large and revolved if needed. The backdrop was a maze of fishing gear such as buoys and nets, etc. We had practiced and practiced our number until we were finally approved and the date set. We were the first to begin the program and when the curtain started to rise I was shocked to see the multitude of faces staring at us. We had no music to which to refer.

36

We had to memorize every note and play it without any error. Looking at the many faces I began to doubt if I would remember all my notes. Before I could think any further the introduction began and we all started to play exactly as we had practiced. This was indeed quite an experience for me to say the least.

Every student studying for the ministry was expected to do some regular Christian service. I joined a small group that went to Clinton every Sunday morning. I chose to teach a Sunday school class in a Methodist Church noted for preaching the gospel. I also led the singing for the morning service. After church, the Pastor invited me to join him and his family for dinner. I can still taste the southern fried chicken, mashed potatoes and vegetables. The desserts were great as well. After dinner, I joined the rest of the group that had done their Christian service in other churches and we all went to the county jail to conduct a service for the inmates. After this service, we drove back to the campus and picked up our bagged lunch of a cheese sandwich and an orange. Later that evening I drove to Gaffney and played the trumpet in a Salvation Army band for their evening service. After the service, I was treated to a welcome snack. After fellowshipping for a short time, I drove back to BJU and prepared for the next day of classes. I repeated this routine for the entire school year.

One of the most exciting and fascinating extracurricular things that I did was to be in a movie film created by the college. Mrs. Stenholm was in charge of the film division of the college and she was looking for volunteers for the upcoming film "Wine of the Morning." This was a film about the life, crucifixion and resurrection of Christ. My roommate, Dick Williams, and I volunteered to be part of the angry crowd in the film that cried out for the crucifixion of Christ. Our lines were quite simple. On cue we had to shout "Crucify Him! Crucify Him!" We were to report to the makeup room at 5:00 am on the day stipulated. They dressed us as rich merchants. They even made a mustache and beard to match my hair color, which was red at that time. After the makeup we went to breakfast. Would you believe we were served pancakes and syrup? You can probably guess what happened to me with my mustache and beard. Yes, you are right; I managed to get syrup all over both the mustache and the beard. What a mess I made of myself. Next we went to the movie site. It looked like we were in the old city of Jerusalem. As we started the shoot a cloud covered the sun. That meant we had to cut production and wait for the cloud to pass. The shoot started again with the familiar: lights, camera, and action. That didn't last very long when a small airplane passed overhead. Once again the command to "cut," was ordered by Mrs. Stenholm. Our scene was finally over and done. Later that week in Preacher Boy Class, (which consisted of about 1,500 men), Mrs. Stenholm came into the class and shared with us that the crowd scene that was shot was great but the shout of "Crucify Him!" was not to her liking. She had the entire class on her command shout: "Crucify Him!" It pleased her and that shout was edited into the film. To this day I have never seen the film. The only evidence that I was in the film is on the DVD of my ministry, which included my days at BJU.

As the year came to a close Dick and I discussed what we would do during the coming summer. We decided to use our musical talents and do some Christian service. Dick belonged to a conservative Baptist Church in Tempe, Arizona, several miles from Phoenix. He wrote to his pastor and he suggested that we write to the Conservative Baptist office in Phoenix and explain what we wanted to do. They in turn furnished us with a list of Conservative Baptist Churches throughout the state of Arizona. We began writing the letters and started to get responses. We laid out a suggested plan of conducting a weekend of services beginning with Friday night and concluding with Sunday evening. One of us would lead the singing, both of us would play our instruments and the other would bring a short message. We received a film about the college that we would show on Saturday night instead of preaching a message. Dean Liverman, Dean of Students, lent us the film. Dick's home church lent us the projector and Dick's dad bought him a new 1954 Ford to use for the meetings.

We received an invitation to be at a camp for boys, many of which were Native American. We even had an invitation to conduct a ten-day meeting in Goodyear, Arizona. This posed a problem because between us we hadn't managed to have that many sermons prepared. We did however arrange somehow to fulfill the invitation. We never asked for money. We did establish that whatever money we received we would set aside to pay for our return trip to BJU. That summer I had a wonderful time living with Dick, his parents and younger brother. It was very difficult to say goodbye when we had to start back to college. His folks welcomed me as one of their own and treated me as if I were their son.

I tried to get a summer job but to no avail until about the second last week of my stay in Arizona. I was able to convince the owner of a brick factory to hire me even if for only two weeks. He warned me that I could not work at the pace that I was used to back east because the heat was greater there and more so in the factory. I watched the Mexicans doing their work and thought I, too, could do just as well. So I began to work hard but it wasn't long until I passed out and woke up in the owner's office. The heat did the job on me and that was that. He paid me for the hours that I worked but said that it wouldn't work out for me on that job. I took my pay, as little as it was, and went back to the Williams' home a little defeated.

Half way through the summer we had a week or two without any scheduled meetings. The Youth Pastor from Dick's church lived in Souderton and he was taking his family back to Souderton for their vacation. I arranged to drive back to Pennsylvania with them. Now I could spend some time with Elaine. She was working and saving her money to pay for her tuition to Berean Bible School but was willing to pay my bus fare back to Phoenix. It was to be a three-day trip by Greyhound bus changing several times. It was the longest and most boring ride I ever had but had good memories of being back with Elaine even if it was just for a short time.

Soon the summer was over and it was time to load the car and head back home to Catasauqua and prepare for the trip back to BJU. Dick and I left his family and his home in Phoenix at night. We decided to change drivers and drive straight through stopping for gas, meals and an oil change. We made it in thirty-three hours. It was preplanned that when I returned at the end of summer I would have my wisdom teeth removed. Dick stayed with me for a few days before he drove back by himself to BJU. I went into Allentown hospital to have my wisdom teeth removed.

I was only home for the procedure for a short time when it was time to say goodbye to my parents, two sisters and Elaine. As I was driving Elaine home I noticed that my ampere gauge indicated that my generator was not charging. By now it was about 10:00 pm and then the only garage I knew that was open 24 hours a day was a truck garage on 18th Street in Allentown. They were kind enough to take care of me and get me on the road again. My funds were low and now even lower after paying the bill. I drove Elaine to her home and kissed her goodbye. It was about midnight when I began my long drive to Greenville, South Carolina. Once again I made the trip in a little over fourteen hours. I was surprised to learn that I would have Dick Williams as my roommate for my sophomore year. We had requested to room together before we left for Arizona and they had honored our request. Like last year there were four bunks in our room but only three of us to the room. Our new roommate was Tom Kalulie from Hawaii.

The next day I registered for my classes and paid about one hundred dollars of my first semester's tuition. I had a little over twenty-five dollars left. Before I started classes I looked around for part-time work to earn enough to pay for my second year of schooling. I started to carry newspapers for the Greenville News. Even though my friend and roommate Dick Williams had his own checkbook and could afford not to work, he also took a paper route. So Dick and I would get up very early in the morning Monday through Friday and carry newspapers. As classes started I once again became active in the Society band, soccer and basketball. It soon occurred to me that carrying newspapers would not be enough to cover my school costs. I found a job stocking shelves at a large grocery chain store near the campus. I worked that job Friday night and Saturday. This still was not sufficient for my expenses so I found a job as a bill collector. I would get a small percentage of the money I collected each day.

My first customer to call on was a poor black lady who had purchased a radio from a department store with a dollar down but failed to make any other payments. When I arrived at her humble cottage I was welcomed by a small boy who didn't seem to have had a bath for some days. The cottage was quite small with a mother of several small children who were running around looking strangely at me. The mother was in bed and had recently given birth to another child. As authoritative as I could sound, although I was deeply moved by all that I was seeing, I announced who I was and that I was a bill collector coming to collect on the radio she had bought but failed to make any payments. Her answer was simply she had no money, her husband was in jail and now she had another mouth to feed. I put on my best disguise and said that I would return in an hour. She had to pay me at least one dollar or I would have to take her radio back to the store. She pleaded with me not to take her radio. I repeated my demand and left. One hour later I returned. The same little dirty boy met me at the door with a fifty-cent piece and fifty dirty pennies. I looked into his dirty face and sad eyes and saw his fist full of coins. I took a deep breath and returned to my car empty handed. My next stop was back to the agency. I told the manager that I was sorry but this job was not for me.

As the days went speedily by I became concerned that if I failed to get up on time in the morning, I would start my paper route late, return back to the college late, miss breakfast and receive some demerits. I found that on several occasions while trying to fall asleep I would start thinking about that scenario. As a result I would awaken with an anxious feeling, jump out of my bunk, awaken Dick and quickly dress. Upon entering the hall of our dormitory, the clock showed 2:00 am. This situation happened several times and as a result, I found myself falling asleep during some of my classes. I knew this couldn't go on and so I called home and received my mother's permission to withdraw from BJU. I went to the Dean's office the next day and completed the transaction. I remember that this all occurred around Thanksgiving time, November 1954. Soon my car was packed and I said a sad farewell to my new-found friend, Dick Williams, and started for home.

High School graduation 1953

Trip to Bob Jones University 1953

Paid $50.00 for my '36 Ford

My first car – 1936 Ford

42

My second car – '42 Plymouth

Roommate Dick
Williams at BJU

Love Birds

BJU Oom Pah Pah Band

Rich merchant in movie
"Wine of the Morning"

Car that Dick Williams'
dad bought

Dick & Dick summer ministry

First Baptist Church,
Goodyear, Arizona

Native American boys camp,
Arizona

# Marriage

I was glad to get home and especially to be with Elaine. Elaine was in her second year of Berean Bible School. She had one more year before she would graduate. She was working afternoons at Roxy Linoleum Company at 18th and Allen Streets and attending classes in the morning. I was able to get an afternoon part-time job at the same place. Roxy Linoleum not only handled floor coverings but was a hardware and toy store as well. Elaine worked with hardware and toys. I would deliver floor covering to the job site and when not doing that would work with hardware and toys with Elaine. In January 1955, I enrolled at Berean Bible School. Some of my BJU credits could be applied so that I would need only 2 1/2 years at Berean.

It wasn't long after beginning my first semester at Berean that I joined the choir and a male quartet was formed. On Sundays the quartet would accompany Rev. Jansen Hartman, President of Berean, when we visited other Mennonite Brethren in Christ churches for their Sunday services. Rev. Hartman would preach and the quartet would sing several numbers. Elaine always accompanied us on these trips. It wasn't long before I proposed to Elaine. I remember asking her father for his permission. His only question to me was: "Will you be able to support her?" I am sure we did not figure out a budget but were most eager to tie the knot. The wedding date was set for June 4th at 2:00 pm. The wedding ceremony would be held at Bethel Mennonite Brethren in Christ Church, 523 N. 8th Street in Allentown. Friday, June 3 was the last day of classes and graduation exercise for the class of 1955. The graduation service was held at Bethel Mennonite Brethren in Christ Church in Allentown. As soon as the program was ended we began our wedding rehearsal.

June 4th finally arrived. The church was almost filled with family, relatives and friends. Rev. Walter Frank preformed the ceremony and Clarence Kauffman played the organ. After the ceremony, we had light refreshments and, of course, the wedding cake in the Fellowship Hall of the church. After the reception was over we packed my 1950

Dodge and began our honeymoon trip. Saying goodbye to my new in-laws and Elaine's twin sisters was a little difficult. Brenda and Beverly thought that I was taking their big sister away and never bringing her back. They stood crying as we pulled away from 523 N. Lumber Street. The total amount we had for our honeymoon trip was exactly $185.00. Our first night was spent at the Roxann Motel somewhere in Maryland. The next day we arrived in Washington, DC. The first motel we checked into was a disaster and we refused the room. We found a much nicer motel a few miles away. After seeing the major tourist sites, we decided to drive to visit Harvey and Bertha Fritz in Greenville, South Carolina. Harvey was completing his Master's degree at BJU. We stayed a day or two with them and discovered that we had spent half of our honeymoon funds so we reasoned that we needed to head back to our new home.

Since we were both students living on a part-time income we couldn't afford to spend much to rent an apartment. My aunt Emily was willing to rent us a sitting room and a bedroom on the second floor of her home at 505 Fairview Street, Coopersburg, for $25.00 a month. So we would leave our new home early in the morning in order to attend our first class at 7:30 am. At first this setup didn't please my mother. She had the idea that we should buy a trailer and move it next to the home of my parents in Catasauqua. We strongly disagreed with her plan and that's why we took Emily's offer.

About this time my mother became ill. After a short period of time we noticed that she was gaining weight and her face became quite puffy. After a doctor's checkup it was discovered that she had tumors growing in her sinus cavities. Arrangements were made for her to be admitted to Harlem Eye Ear and Nose Hospital in New York City. The doctors skillfully removed the tumors without disturbing her face. After a short stay she returned home. However, the tumors began growing in other parts of her body. At the same time I left Roxy Linoleum Company and started working at Cassie's Sunoco Gas Station on Front Street in Catasauqua. This now changed our daily schedule.

After our classes at Berean Bible School we would get a bite to eat. I took Elaine to Roxy Linoleum to work in the afternoon while I returned to Berean and went to the Library to do my homework or practice with the quartet. After I picked up Elaine we went to Catasauqua where Elaine would spend time with my ailing mother and complete her homework while I worked at Cassie's Sunoco gas station from 5:00 pm to 10:00 pm. After I was finished working Elaine and I would drive to Coopersburg and settle in for the night. This we did from Monday to Friday. On Saturday, I worked a full day at Cassie's Sunoco Station. Here I learned to service cars, put on new brakes and do tune ups. I also washed cars in between pumping gas. It got a little rough in the winter time. Not when I was washing cars or servicing them indoors but in the winter when a gas customer came into the station I had to run outside to pump gas, clean windows and check the oil level. My hands became rough, chapped and cracked open in spots.

Every Sunday while in Berean Elaine and the rest of the quartet would pile in my car and we would follow Rev. Hartman and some other students to attend Sunday Services throughout the Mennonite Brethren in Christ Conference. That June Elaine graduated from Berean with the class of 1956. Elaine left Roxy Linoleum and took a job as a secretary at Allentown Paint Company in Allentown. June of 1957 I graduated from Berean and we moved from Coopersburg to Ridge Ave. and Gordon Streets in Allentown. I had found a small third floor apartment. It was a little unusual because we had to climb out the kitchen window and step down a foot onto the roof below to hang up the wash. It was at this time that I enrolled at the Wesleyan College in Allentown and took a full-time job at the Lehigh Valley Dairy. I had classes in the morning and would work an eight-hour shift in the ice cream department beginning anytime from noon to 6:00 pm. My job was to help in the packaging of the ice cream for about four hours and then after the run was completed for the day we would tear down the stainless-steel pipes and packaging machines, thoroughly cleaning them with a special dairy soap and high pressure water. On lighter production days I would start at noon and get home before nine at night. On Thursday which was the heaviest production day I would

48

start at six pm and wouldn't be home until closer to three am. After my shift I would do my class assignments for the next day.

It was during my first year at the Wesleyan College that my mother became seriously ill with lymphoma cancer. The only treatment available was the cobalt treatment offered at Sacred Heart Hospital in Allentown. She rapidly declined and was admitted to Sacred Heart Hospital. In only a few short days she passed away and was buried at the Mennonite Brethren in Christ Church cemetery in Coopersburg.

Our little third floor apartment on Ridge & Gordon soon became undesirable. It wasn't long after our move that Elaine gave birth to a tiny beautiful baby girl born January 14, 1958. We named her Roxann Elaine. Shortly after Roxann's arrival we were able to rent a more suitable apartment from Bethel Mennonite Brethren in Christ Church on N. 8th Street. It became much easier to drop into the Metzger's now because all we had to do was walk across the alley behind our apartment.

Berean Bible School

Berean Bible School quartet

1957 Class reunion

Berean Bible School graduation

Our wedding
June 4, 1955

With our
parents

Bride and Groom

Getting away before the reception

Wedding reception

Big sister with Brenda
and Beverly

Honeymoon at the
Roxann Motel

Lincoln Memorial

Visiting Harvey and
Bertha in Greenville, SC

Aunt Emily

First apartment at Aunt
Emily's in Coopersburg

Daughter Roxann born
1-14-58

# Jersey City

While attending the Wesleyan College I accepted a call to pastor a small country church, Mountain View Chapel, near Pottstown, PA. I pastored the church for about a year and a half after which I began my ministry with the Bible Fellowship Church's Church Extension Department (the name change from Mennonite Brethren in Christ to Bible Fellowship had happened earlier that year). Under the Bible Fellowship Church, you were assigned a church. This took place at their Annual Conference which was always held in the month of October. On Friday of the Conference we were notified where we would serve as pastor. We were appointed to a mission church in Jersey City and were expected to be in the pulpit the following Sunday. On Saturday grandma watched Roxann while Elaine and I drove to Jersey City to familiarize ourselves with our new home.

Berean Bible Fellowship Church, 45 Lincoln Street, Jersey City was our new home. It was a converted factory building, thirty feet wide and one hundred feet long. Our living quarters were upstairs on the second floor. It consisted of a foyer, a small family room, a sufficient dining room, small kitchen with a long hall leading to a large thirty by thirty-foot room. Connecting the front room to the large back room was a long hall where a bathroom and several bedrooms were located. The hall was long enough to become a bowling alley. Several of our friends gave us their unused bedroom suites and we had enough furnished bedrooms to host visitors.

Bob McIntyre was the previous pastor and had invited us to come to Jersey City the Saturday prior to our first service the next day. Bob would show us around the building and bring us up to date on the church. He would himself have to be in Paradise, PA the next day to preach his first sermon at the Paradise, PA Bible Fellowship Church.

Bob gave us a thorough tour, pointing out all the negative things about the building. We started on the second floor. The thirty-foot by thirty-foot backroom was used primarily for the Ladies Missionary

Fellowship that met monthly. I noticed walking around the room that there were X marks on the floor here and there. He told me that when it rained, the roof leaked. He then took me into the little kitchen in the corner of the room and opening a cabinet door he took out one of the big pots from the shelf and said he would place this pot and others from the cabinet on the X's to catch the dripping rain water. Next we went into the basement. On the way down the stairs the sewer pipe ran against the wall and out to the street. He pointed out that there was a crack in the pipe and sometimes it would leak sewage onto the floor. He then continued to explain about the aging furnace. Rust would build up in the furnace and periodically in the winter the water with the rust needed to be drained out and a new supply of water added to the boiler.

Continuing back upstairs to the living quarters he spent considerable time explaining about the makeup of the congregation. There were 22 enrolled in Sunday school. A person attending Sunday school for three consecutive Sundays was automatically enrolled. Several elderly people lived a short distance from the church and usually walked to church. Some folks were picked up by the pastor and driven to church.

That evening as Elaine and I went to bed we talked a little about what took place earlier that day. This was going to be a hard adjustment for Elaine. She had never spent any amount of time away from her home and the surroundings of Allentown. I was quite sad about the situation I was bringing her and Roxann into and I actually began to cry.

Sunday arrived and we met the families of our congregation for the first time. We were warmly welcomed. Mr. Wright became the spokesman and would later spend some time with me adding his point of view on the church.

Plans were being made for our move to Jersey City. The Bible Fellowship Conference had a system of moving the pastors from one assignment to another. First the movers came to our apartment in Allentown and loaded our furniture, etc. When the movers arrived in Jersey City they unloaded our belongings. They next loaded Bob &

Marilyn's furniture on the truck to be delivered the next day to Paradise, PA.

Being assigned to Jersey City made my father-in-law very happy. Earl always loved New York City and now that we were living across the Hudson River visiting the Big Apple would be a real temptation. Earl and Myrtle and the twins would periodically spend a weekend with us. We had several bedrooms for visitors so everyone in the Metzger family had their own bedroom. Elaine's folks would arrive on Friday evening and leave for home on Sunday afternoon. Earl and I would usually drive to Journal Square in Jersey City and park in the parking garage above the subway station. We would board the subway and within about a half hour we would be in the New York subway station only a few blocks from Times Square.

We would walk around Times Square sometimes just standing on the sidewalk watching the sea of people walking hurriedly past us. Sometimes we would have a meal at Tad's Steak House in the Times Square area. We would get their special. It consisted of a steak, baked potato and a salad for $1.19. Other times we would walk down to Madison Square Garden and across the street on the corner of 33rd and 7th Avenue. Earl would order a turkey sandwich and a cup of coffee. I went next door and bought a gyro and a coke.

We never had a set pattern to make our way around the city. If we walked up town toward Central Park we could stop at a Horn and Hardart. Here we could look at a large assortment of pies behind a glass window. You would pick the piece you wanted and insert a quarter in the slot. This would automatically unlock the glass door and you could reach in to take out your choice of pie. Coffee was also available. We would take our selection of pie and coffee, and then find a table to sit down and enjoy the snack.

After leaving the Horn and Hardart café we would walk along the edge of Central Park from 59th Street to 8th Avenue. By now we were getting tired. We took the 8th Avenue subway downtown to Canal Street. Our next stop was our favorite Chinese restaurant on Mott

Street. After eating our evening meal and walking around Chinatown we would walk from there to the financial district to take a subway back to Journal Square in Jersey City.

Over the many years, even when we were no longer pastoring in Jersey City, Earl and I would make many such trips to the Big Apple.

Earl and I were very fortunate to have many opportunities to do and see unusual things while I was pastoring in Jersey City and in our other trips to New York City. While I was pastoring in Jersey City Earl and I had the opportunity to ride on the Lehigh Valley Railroad tugboat. Mr. Height, the husband of one of the members of the church, was an oiler on the Lehigh Valley Railroad tugboat. He arranged with the captain of the tugboat to take us on board with him as guests. Earl always took his vacation in August. That August Earl and I boarded the tugboat at midnight. For the next eight hours we towed barges filled with railroad cars up and down the Hudson River. The captain of the tug welcomed us and took us on a tour of the boat. We were free to go anywhere on the tug we wanted to go. The only thing we could not do was ask to steer the tug. The captain also told us that when we were pulling a barge that we should not go outside of the cabin on the side of the tow. There was movement between the tug and the barge and we would be splashed and get wet.

About three o'clock in the morning Earl decided to eat his sandwich while he was sitting in the cabin. He had only taken a few bites when he decided to take his sandwich outside and watch the lights along the river. I warned him about what the captain had told us about going outside while we were towing a barge. That didn't matter to Earl and as he took a few steps outside, he opened his mouth to take a bite of his sandwich as the barge movement caused Earl to get splashed in his face.

Over the years even after leaving Jersey City Earl and I continued to visit the Big Apple. We watched the Twin Towers being built. After they were built we took the elevator to the 107th floor of World Tower

One to the observation deck. It is hard to describe how far you could see at this height. It was an awesome experience.

On one of Earl's birthdays we went to New York City and this time we went to the second Twin Tower and had a cup of coffee and some pastry in the Windows of the World Restaurant. All the seating area was on different levels so that everyone could look out of the windows and see the Hudson River, the Statue of Liberty and Staten Island.

It was around 1976 when Earl and I returned to New York City for a day of sightseeing. One of our stops early in the day was to go to the basement coffee shop of one of New York's elegant hotels. I can't remember the name of the hotel but I do remember that particular day traffic around the hotel was very sparse.

As we drew nearer to the coffee shop entrance we saw policemen on horseback and men in suits walking around with ear pierces and talking into their sleeves. We soon learned that these were secret service men and President Jimmy Carter was inside. Outside the hotel, parked at the curb, was the President's specially built Cadillac. I asked permission for Earl and me to look inside through one of the windows. Permission was granted. The instrument panel was not a standard Cadillac instrument panel and dashboard. Many more gauges and switches were visible. We were allowed to spend just a few minutes taking in the awesomeness of the car. We thanked the secret service agent and went into the coffee shop for our usual first cup of New York coffee. We used this coffee shop because it had clean restrooms. After enjoying our coffee we walked down the hallway to the men's room. As we left the coffee shop we noticed we were walking on red carpet with a lot of heavy wires running along the baseboard. At the corridor where the restroom was located there were several New York City policemen standing in various places around the corridor. After using the restroom I walked over to one of the policemen and asked about all the security, etc. we had noticed outside the Hotel. He told me that Jimmy Carter was scheduled to come down the elevator and leave through the corridor we were standing in. After a few minutes of talking with him he told us to step back near the wall and wait for him to give us the signal. Time passed rapidly and soon he nodded and the elevator door opened and Jimmy Carter stepped out in front of us. He smiled and extended his hand so that both Earl and I had the opportunity of shaking the hand of Jimmy Carter, President of the USA. This of course was the highlight of our day.

One of the church members of First Baptist Church in Phillipsburg, Ron Smith had been in the control tower of Kennedy Airport in NYC. He arranged for Earl and I to be allowed to be in the tower and observe the attendants direct the air traffic.

When we arrived at the tower we had to pick up the phone and identify ourselves. The door had an electric lock and we heard the buzz as the door opened. We were able to spend some time in the tower and observe all that occurs when a plane is about to land or to take off. We then were taken to the radar room to see how many planes were actually in the sky. We were invited to come back and it was suggested that coming at night would offer a great view with all the lights on the runways. Earl and I actually made the trip to the control tower on several more occasions including a night trip.

Ron Smith had transferred from Kennedy Airport to the old Allentown, Bethlehem, and Easton airport control tower. Once again he arranged for Earl and me to be able to go inside that tower and observe the air traffic flow. It was an interesting experience but nothing like our tours of the control tower at Kennedy airport.

Now back to when we moved to Jersey City. We began our ministry in Jersey City on October 1959. I began visiting people and making friends with our new neighbors. To the right of the church were Mr. & Mrs. Houghton. They operated Houghton's funeral home. To the left of the church were two brothers who pretty much kept to themselves. Their next-door neighbor was a policeman on the Jersey City police force. Next to the policeman was an oil truck driver. Mr. Houghton, the policeman and the truck driver would come to the church and sit on the steps. I would join them and we would talk about many topics. We decided to call ourselves the Lincoln Street Council. Mr.

Houghton was the President and the policeman was the sergeant of arms. Roxann won their hearts and many evenings about 7:00 pm Mr. Softie's ice cream truck came down the street. Mr. Houghton or one of the other council members would purchase a small cone for Roxann. Sometimes she was getting ready for bed but they would insist that she needed to have her ice cream treat. She earned the nickname of Miss 55. If you ask her what something costs she would always respond with "55."

We began to see an increase in Sunday school and church attendance. It was getting to be a problem picking up people in my 1957 Plymouth 2 door sedan. A Christian businessman in Allentown who was following our ministry had a 1958 Plymouth three-seat station wagon. He was going to buy a new car to replace the station wagon and wanted to know if his station wagon would fit better into our purposes at the church. He told me to sell my car and then he would sell me his station wagon at a very low cost. A couple in our church needed a car and bought my car. I used the station wagon to pick up people for Sunday school and Church.

About this time we were having some young boys attending Sunday school and church. I began a Boys' Brigade program and the station wagon fit the program quite well. I took the boys to Camp Bethel for a weekend retreat. We could fit everything into the station wagon. Joe Beam, a professional cook and a member of Bethel Church, volunteered to be our cook for the retreat. I had worked out the schedule for the weekend which would include a hike through the woods on Saturday morning after breakfast. We would return to the lodge for lunch. After lunch we would swim in the stream. However my plan didn't go as expected. I simply got lost in the thick woods. When I hunted at Camp Bethel I was told that if I lost my direction I should walk in as straight a line as possible until I came to a barbed wire fence or a stream. I was to follow the barbed wire fence in either direction and I would eventually come to a road. If I came to the stream I was to follow the flow of the water and I would come to a road. If I missed either the barbed wire fence or the stream I would eventually end up in Wilkes Barre. With the boys following me I

60

found the stream and followed it back to the camp. Instead of having lunch at noon we ate at 2:00 pm.

As time went on, the cost to operate the station wagon was quite high. On one of my trips back to Allentown I had lunch with the Christian businessman and he began to ask me about the station wagon and the expense to run it. He suggested that I should go back to Jersey City and get a quote for a new 1960 Valiant, and he would do the same here in the Lehigh Valley. I followed through and sent him the quote. Time went by and one day I received a phone call from him asking me if I would be coming back to Allentown soon. We would come back to Allentown at least once a month. Living in Jersey City for Elaine was quite an adjustment and she became homesick. When this would occur we would leave on Sunday after the evening service and stay with her folks until Monday evening and then return back to Jersey City. It was on one of these trips back home that the Christian businessman told me to bring the title to the station wagon because he had purchased a new 1960 Valiant for us. All the way on our trip back to Allentown we were trying to guess what the color was. We knew we only wanted standard shift and a radio. What a surprise we had when we saw the new car. It was white with black and silver checked seats. It was a 4-door sedan and had enough room to meet our needs.

The congregation continued to grow. Now I had several able men who were willing to go up on the roof and make repairs so that the large backroom would be dry in a rain storm. The backroom now was not only used for Ladies Missionary Fellowship but also for Boys' Brigade. I repainted the floor and painted in a shuffle board area.

As the congregation increased in size so also did the giving. We were now ready to think about supporting a missionary. Every quarter we held a congregational business meeting when the Church Extension Director would serve as chairman and I would be the secretary. It was at a quarterly business meeting after reviewing the increases in attendance and giving, that we requested the Bible Fellowship Conference to assign a missionary to us that we could partially support, pray for and communicate with. We were assigned Roy and

61

Diane Hertzog, missionaries with the Voice of Tangier later named Trans World Radio (TWR). They would be serving in Tangier, Morocco.

A short time later we received word that the Hertzogs would be sailing from New York City to begin their ministry. A farewell service was planned for those who could attend as they left to begin their assignment. The day came and Elaine bundled up Roxann who was about 2 years old. It was the dead of winter and bitterly cold when we parked the car at the foot of 42nd Street just a short distance from where the ship was docked. When the farewell service ended we said our goodbyes and made our way back to the car. To our amazement we were the only car parked on that side of the street. As we drew closer I could see a piece of paper attached to the windshield wiper on the driver's side. It didn't take me long to see that it was a parking ticket for $25.00. That was a lot of money for that day and more of a jolt because we only had a $28.00 balance in the checkbook. The next payday was two weeks away. Naturally, we paid the ticket. The next time we communicated with the Hertzogs I had to tell them this story. Even today we each chuckle about the time the Hertzogs almost wiped us out financially when we joined with them on the day they set sail for their ministry.

We had been in Jersey City now for about a year and a half. We had more than doubled in attendance and I began to look at different areas to which we might relocate. About the same time the Church Extension Director informed me that the Church Extension Department leadership had decided to close the church in Jersey City and move us to Belvidere, New Jersey to start a new church. The church building in Jersey City was in very bad condition and not worth investing any more money to do the multitude of repairs. This came as a shock to the congregation. However there were a least three good churches in the area that they could begin to attend. So after serving in Jersey City for about one and a half years we moved to Belvidere, NJ.

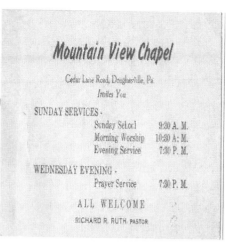

**Mountain View Chapel**

Cedar Lane Road, Douglasville, Pa.

*Invites You*

SUNDAY SERVICES -

| | |
|---|---|
| Sunday School | 9:30 A. M. |
| Morning Worship | 10:30 A: M. |
| Evening Service | 7:30 P. M. |

WEDNESDAY EVENING -

| | |
|---|---|
| Prayer Service | 7:30 P. M. |

ALL WELCOME

RICHARD R. RUTH PASTOR

Mt. View Chapel, Douglasville, PA – First church I pastored

Berean Bible Fellowship
Church, Jersey City, NJ

First family portrait at Jersey City

Snowstorm, Jersey City

Mrs. Wright, organist at Jersey City

Mrs. Bayshore, pianist, Jersey City

My father-in-law, my New York traveling buddy

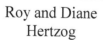

Roy and Diane Hertzog

# Belvidere

The Church Extension Director had received a request from several people in Belvidere that they wanted to start a church there. He arranged to have a tent erected on the school property and conducted children's meetings in the morning and evangelistic services in the evening. At the end of that week 60 people said they were interested to see a church organized in Belvidere. This situation was the deciding factor in the demise of Jersey City mission and the beginning of a new church plant in Belvidere. Elaine and I were appointed to begin this process. The congregation of Jersey City was able to find another church to join several blocks away.

We moved to 506 Water Street in Belvidere, NJ sometime during the summer months. I am not sure what the exact date was. Our apartment was on the second floor but was quite small. We had a very small kitchen that when we sat around the table to eat a meal you could not open the oven or the refrigerator doors. There was a small living room, bath and bedroom on that floor. The attic was a small finished room that became my office. The church services were held in the old firehouse on Water Street. Water Street was the main street through Belvidere that went from Riverton, PA through Belvidere and joined Route 46. So we always had lots of traffic going past our apartment.

Elaine was pregnant with Rick when we moved from Jersey City to Belvidere. It wasn't long after moving to Belvidere that Elaine gave birth to a handsome boy on February 20, 1962. We named him Richard R. Ruth II, but we nicknamed him Ricky. Elaine had considerable difficulty with both of the births of Roxann and Rick. With Roxann's birth Elaine was confined to bed rest for 6 months. With Rick she hemorrhaged and we almost lost her. We are so thankful to the Lord for His watchful care over Elaine and the fact that we have been blessed with two wonderful children.

After we unpacked our belongings I began to visit each one of the 60 people that said they would be interested in establishing a church.

After visiting each one I learned that there was only one that would actually be committed to start the church. On our first Sunday in the firehouse there was the Church Extension Director, his wife and two boys, myself, Elaine, Roxann and Ricky and the one committed person. We didn't have a pianist so all of our singing was done acapella.

Over time I was able to meet more of the residents of Belvidere and invite them to our services. I frequented the town bakery for coffee and a doughnut and at the coffee shop next to the post office or "This'll do us coffee shop." I became friends with the owner of the Route 46 truck stop. Many Sunday nights I would drive there for some hamburgers and bring them back for a late supper. I established a friendship with the members of the fire company. Every service we had at the firehouse auditorium required that we set up chairs, etc. and after the service take down the chairs and stack them in their storage space. The old upright piano that belonged to the fire company was painted silver and was placed on a small elevated platform. Our Sunday service was a combined service, meaning that we included songs that would be sung in Sunday school, a short Bible lesson, either a hymn or two and a sermon. The service would be an hour and a half in length.

The interesting thing about meeting for church in the Goodwill Fire Company of Belvidere, NJ was that our meeting room was directly behind the garage that housed the fire truck and fire equipment. Only a thin wall separated the fire truck from our meeting room. On top of the roof directly over our meeting room was positioned the siren that was used for ambulance and fire calls. If I was conducting a service in the meeting room and there was a call for either ambulance or fire, the siren blasted off loud and clear. It was so loud that the only thing to do was to wait until the siren stopped before going on with the service. However, the other problem with which to contend besides the sound of the siren was that many of the men attending the service either were a member of the ambulance corps or a fireman. So, when the siren blew and I was conducting the service I had to first stop speaking and watch the men disappear out the door. Next, I had to decide if I should jump on the fire truck and conclude the message or just wait until the commotion was over.

I am not clear as to how we contacted Bob Allshouse, but he was asked to come and play the piano for our services. He was an excellent musician and fit in well with our small and growing congregation. It was amazing that after a short time playing the old piano that Elaine introduced Bob to my younger sister, Lois. After some time in courting, Bob proposed and Bob and Lois were married.

Jim and Goldie Alexander began attending the church. He saw that we really needed a communion table with storage space for hymnals. He built a wonderful communion table and a matching pulpit. More and more people came and became a faithful part of the church family. We scheduled special meetings throughout the year beginning on Friday night and ending on Sunday night. I contacted Andy Telford, a well-known Bible teacher, and some other professors from Philadelphia College of the Bible to be our special speakers. We continued to see steady growth.

In the summer, we received permission from a wonderful couple who owned 3 1/2 acres on Pequest Road, across the street from Belvidere High School, to erect a tent for special meetings. We borrowed a large tent from the Bible Fellowship Conference and erected it on this piece of property. I had several men to help erect the tent, build a platform and build seating. Rev. and Mrs. Robert Smock conducted children's meetings in the morning and I arranged to have a special friend of mine, who was an excellent speaker, for the evening services. His name was Rev. Robert Brooks from Landrum, South Carolina. I met him while I was a student at Bob Jones University. My mother had bought me a Webcor reel-to-reel recorder that had a built in public address system. Allen Musselman from Bethel Bible Fellowship Church in Allentown was the one who ran all the wires and hooked up the speakers for Mizpah Grove Camp meeting services. When Mizpah ended these services, Allen had acquired the speakers. He graciously loaned them to me for our tent meetings. I hooked up the speakers to my Webcor P.A. system and that served us well as our sound system.

We had good attendance at both the children's meetings and evening evangelistic services. This added more people and interest to our services held at the firehouse. We ran these tent meetings for several summers and always held them either before or after the other churches in town ran their DVBS. We didn't want to cause any undue friction with the churches in town. Our attendances were so good that the churches in town asked me if we would include them the next year because their attendances were very small running the traditional DVBS meetings. This never occurred because in the fall of that same year 1964, I became quite ill and eventually resigned from the church. But let's get back to where we left off.

We arrived in Belvidere in 1961 and by 1963 we had almost filled the firehouse auditorium to capacity. We began to look around for some property to build a church building. At the same time there was a rumor around town that a large pharmaceutical company was looking for property to build a large plant. No one was interested in our request to consider selling us several acres to build a church. However, when I asked to see the older couple that had allowed us to erect a tent on their property for the last few summers, they would allow me to visit them but really weren't interested in selling the property. They were both school teachers and wanted to begin a nursery on that property when they retired. We had a good meeting and I asked them again if they would consider selling the property to the church. They said they would give it some thought but they really wanted to build a nursery there.

I can't recall how long after my meeting with them that I received a call inviting me to meet with them to talk about the property. The whole congregation was praying for a place to build the church and knew that if this was God's will for us to build a church building in Belvidere that a piece of property would become available. I earnestly prayed for God's will before I reached their home. They greeted me at the door and before I could get in the door they said in unison they thought it over and wanted us to have the property.

The congregation was delighted with the good news. Our hopes were high as we considered that we would have a church building in God's timing. The first thing we did was to establish a building fund to raise the necessary funds to purchase the property. While this was in progress we needed to decide about finding an architect to discuss the church building. For some reason known only to the Lord, I was at the lumber yard in Washington, NJ and began talking to one of the clerks about our desire to build a church in Belvidere. In the course of our conversation he mentioned an architect from Patterson, NJ that uses steel structure to build several kinds of buildings. I took down his name and phone number. As soon as I returned home that day I made a call to him. His name was Dominic Lentini and in the course of our conversation I found out that he was a believer and very interested in meeting with me. That meeting was scheduled just a few days after the initial phone conversation.

Ed and Bert O'Neil were regular attenders at our church and he was very familiar with the building trade having built a home or two over the years. He was very willing to be a member of the building committee. In fact he and I were the only members.

Bud and Barbara Smith were our next-door neighbors and began attending with their two girls. Their daughters became regular playmates with Roxann. Barb Smith's father, Erwin Smith, was a draftsman for Pfizer Chemical Company in Easton and willingly was available to assist us in any way. In speaking with Mr. Lentini he was agreeable to our suggestion that Erwin Smith would do the drawings under Dominic's supervision. So this was the plan: I would drive Ed O'Neil and Erwin Smith down to Patterson to meet with Dominic at his home. Together Ed and Dominic would discuss the dimensions and plans for the building. Erwin Smith would take down notes and after the discussion we would drive back to Belvidere. Mr. Smith would begin to work on the drawings. When he had a section competed he would call me and I would in turn call Dominic to set up our next meeting. When it came time to meet, Ed O'Neil, Mr. Smith and I would again drive to Patterson to meet with Dominic to discuss the next phase for Mr. Smith to do the drawings. Time after time we repeated this procedure until finally all the drawings were complete. At this point Dominic checked over each sheet of the drawings carefully and when completed with any corrections, he signed his name and attached his seal. The prints were now ready for a contractor to bid on the construction.

When I first contacted Dominic Lentini, discussed the project and how Ed and Mr. Smith would contribute, I also asked what his fee would be. He graciously said that we would discuss this when the drawings were complete. Now that the drawings were complete, checked over and stamped, it was time to ask Dominic what we now owed him for all that he did for us. To our utter amazement he said that our bill would be $175.00. You can imagine how shocked we were at that low figure but at the same time rejoicing that we were able to gladly pay it. We also gave him as a special gift something that he always wanted for his use around his home. It was a special electric drill. He was very happy to receive the gift and he expressed to us how pleased he was to have met us and enjoyed the many sessions discussing the drawings at his home.

It was after the completion of the drawings that I became quite ill. I made several trips to our family doctor in Belvidere. Instead of improving, I was getting worse. Dr. Marlot told me not to climb the stairs but to sleep and rest on the sofa. I became weaker and weaker finding it very difficult to stand up. Finally, on a Sunday morning Elaine called Dr. Marlot to come to the house. Upon his arrival, he immediately called for the ambulance to transport me to Warren Hospital in Philipsburg. Belvidere's ambulance crop was operated by volunteers. To my surprise Ed O'Neil and Speedy Griffin, both members of the church, responded to the call and they transported me to Warren Hospital. I asked Speedy Griffin who was an excellent Bible teacher to take the service for that Sunday.

I would become so cold that I would shiver for long periods of time and ask for more blankets. Next, I would become extremely hot and want to take the covers off. After several tests and a stay in the hospital for ten days I was released. To this day it was not known what actually caused my illness. It was thought that it could have been malaria or hepatitis. To this day we do not know what actually happened and every blood test taken since then shows no signs of either malaria or hepatitis.

Elaine pregnant
with Ricky

Ricky born 2-20-62

Bob Allshouse, first
pianist at Belvidere NJ,
later married my sister
Lois

Tent services

Bob Brooks
object lesson at
kid's meeting

Belvidere BFC

Family Portrait

# Driving a Truck

When I arrived in Belvidere, Speedy Griffin was an electrical contractor. About two years after our arrival, Speedy expanded his business and went into the trucking business as well. Imco Container was a plastic manufacturing company based in Belvidere. Their main product was the production of plastic bottles for various commodities. Speedy signed a contract to supply trucks and drivers to transport the empty plastic bottles to various distributors and warehouses.

Speedy asked me to drive with him to Philadelphia to purchase his first tractor. He would drive the tractor back to Belvidere and I would follow with his car. Sometime after this he purchased a second tractor. Months later he asked me if I wanted to ride along with him to deliver plastic bottles to Mennen Shaving Company in Morristown, NJ. After we unloaded and returned to Imco's lot, Speedy did not back the trailer into the dock but rather parked the truck in an open space and told me to trade seats with him. As I sat in the driver's seat he began to instruct me on how to shift the 8-speed road ranger transmission, parking tips, etc. Next he told me to drive the rig around the lot and practice backing up. This began a series of driving lessons and finally driving on the road. By now Speedy had acquired several more tractors and had hired several drivers.

Once in a while on a Friday night, one of the trucks was scheduled to deliver a load of bottles to a warehouse in Baltimore, MD. I would be asked to accompany the driver to make the run. He would pull up near our home and blow the horn. That was my signal that he was waiting for me. I jumped into the passenger seat and we drove to the truck stop on Rt. 46 just outside of Belvidere. The driver would fill the tank with diesel fuel and walk around to the passenger side of the truck, open the door and tell me to take the wheel. I would drive the rig to Esther's truck stop on old Rt. 22 where we would have some coffee and a sandwich. I would continue to drive to the warehouse in Baltimore and the return trip back home. This gave me actual driving experience.

After my return from my stay in Warren Hospital I had quite a hospital bill. Our salary was $2,000.00 a year. We lived in a parsonage rent free but we did not have hospitalization. I didn't know how I was going to pay the hospital bill because we had two children and with our normal expenses it was very difficult to make ends meet. We were unable to save any money and lived from week to week. Elaine's parents gave gifts periodically and we would receive produce from Foster and Dorothy Myers who were members of the church and had a farm in Columbia, NJ. Someone even bought us a set of tires for our car when they saw how bald the tires were.

Ron Mahurin and I entered the Church Extension ministry at the Annual Conference of the Bible Fellowship Church, in October 1959. I was stationed in Jersey City and Ron went to Denville, NJ. Our church was an old factory building 30' X 100', and Ron's congregation met in the Denville Public Library. We had several extra bedrooms that were available for friends and family when they would visit us. Ron, his wife, Darlene, and sons, Ronnie and Timmy, would periodically visit with us for the day since Denville was not too far from Jersey City. On one particular occasion when they came for a visit we convinced them to say overnight. When we got up the next morning we were in the midst of a severe snowstorm. All the roads were blocked and no traffic was moving. So Ron and his family stayed with us, believe it or not, for several days. Ron missed having a church service because he was snowed in with us. In fact, the National Guard used one of their tanks to open up our street. Finally, Ron loaded his family into his white 1957 Dodge station wagon and drove home to Denville. We really had a great time those several days.

By the time we were in full swing at Belvidere, Ron's congregation was involved in a church building project. A concrete block company from Center Valley was willing to donate all the concrete blocks needed for their church building but they would have to make arrangements to have them delivered. Rev. Bill Heffner, the Church Extension Director asked me if the Conference would rent a tractor trailer, would I be willing to go to Center Valley, have them load the trailer and deliver them to the building site. I was more than happy to be of service and actually made several trips for the Denville Church construction project. Since the contractor did not have a fork lift to unload the blocks, it had to be done by hand. After the last load was unloaded the contractor asked me if I thought that I could drive to the railroad yard and line up the trailer alongside a railroad flat car that was carrying the church arches. He did not have a big enough truck to be able to truck the arches back to the building site. Believe it or not, there was enough space for me to pull up right next to the railroad car. The truck bed and the railroad car bed were equal in height. We were able to lift one arch at a time, set it on rollers and roll it onto the trailer bed. With this project done I returned the truck and trailer to the rental company and called it a day well spent.

One day soon after I returned from the hospital, Speedy asked me if I would consider driving for him on my day off every week. If I was listed to make a delivery and something came up that I was needed for church business, Speedy said that I should take care of my church responsibilities and he would see that the delivery was made. This would give me extra money to pay my hospital expenses. I then asked my board members for their opinion. Everyone was in agreement with the arrangements made between me and Speedy. So on my day off I would take a load of plastic bottles to Morristown or Jersey City and on a few occasions to the warehouse in Baltimore, MD. I was slowly getting back my full strength. I started talking with the Church Extension Director about the possibility of allowing us to begin to build the church. Soon after speaking with him I received a phone call from Rev. A.L. Seifert, one of the Conference District Superintendents. He requested that I have all the men of the church accompany me to a meeting at Berean Bible School in Allentown, PA. The meeting was set and I arrived with all the men of the church. The meeting was to discuss our request to begin construction of the new church building. District Superintendents, Rev. A.L. Seifert and Rev. T.D. Gehret were present at the meeting but the Church Extension Director was not available to attend the meeting.

The meeting was opened with prayer and Rev. T.D. Gehret began the session by saying that the Conference felt that we were not quite ready to begin the construction. In fact he said they were concerned that I was driving truck and this was frowned upon since the Conference rule was that the Pastor was to live on what he was paid. So their instruction to us was to wait on the building program. With this the meeting was ended and we were thanked for making the trip. As we were leaving I was asked to remain behind. After the men had left the room I was instructed that I had six weeks to stop driving the truck or they would remove me from Belvidere.

The next day after this meeting I went to the terminal manager and told him about the meeting and my instructions to stop driving after six weeks. I requested to be put on the list full-time. I drove as often as I was listed to drive and after six weeks I stopped driving. Driving more than one day a week allowed me to raise enough money to pay all my hospital expenses. Even though I drove more days than one for that period of time, it didn't hinder my church responsibilities.

That summer I was obligated to attend the Bible Fellowship Camp Meeting in South Allentown. All Pastors of the Bible Fellowship denomination were expected to be in attendance for the setting up of the grove and to be in attendance for another week when the morning and evening services were conducted. The first week was erecting the tents, cleaning the auditorium and restrooms and placing the benches in the auditorium. I was one of the piano moving crew as well as driving in stakes with a sledge hammer to secure the tent ropes.

I was approached by one of the older Pastors during the first week of services. He said that he had heard good reports about the ministry in Belvidere and the steady growth of the church. But he was alarmed by the report that I was driving a truck. This was something definitely opposed by the Conference. He asked if I had learned any lessons through this past year since I thought I needed to drive a truck. My answer simply was yes I had. He asked me again, "what did you learn?" I responded that if I ever got into a financial bind again I would be like the Apostle Paul and go make tents. This was not the answer he had expected and he as much as told me so in words and actions.

Soon after the Camp Meeting session I returned to Belvidere and still remained feeling weak. After several visits to the doctor it was suggested by the doctor that for my health and my family's well-being, that I leave the ministry until I was able to once again have full strength. I followed his suggestion and notified the Church Extension Director that I would submit my resignation to be effective at the October Annual Conference session.

Soon after I submitted my resignation from the church in Belvidere, Ken and June Brobst of Forks Township in Easton, invited us for an evening meal. Ken and June were both music teachers in the Easton School District and very personal friends of ours for many years. They would be our special music every year we had the tent meeting at Belvidere.

The day came for us to go to the Brobst's for supper. We left Belvidere early. We arrived near the Brobst's house but I missed the street that I was to turn to their home. They lived on Ridge Terrace and I drove past the street that I should have turned on. We turned off of Old Mill Road onto George Street and at the corner of Apple Blossom Road and George Street was a cute little Cape Cod house with a sign on the lawn that read: "For sale by owner." Since we were early for supper we decided to ask to see the house. We immediately fell in love with it. After a fast tour we made our way to Ken and June's home for the evening meal. We were excited about the house we just went through and shared our enthusiasm with our friends. It was most of our conversation that night.

Since I was no longer the Pastor of the Belvidere church, I found a job with Joe Beers driving a ten-wheel dump truck. I made an appointment to talk with John Frenzi, a real estate agent in Easton about purchasing the house at 500 Apple Blossom Rd and George Street. I had a life insurance policy that had a cash value of $500.00. I withdrew the money and used it as a down payment.

After I began driving for Joe Beers I was asked to drive a day or two a week for Bieter's Transfer Company in Alpha, NJ. When I drove a tractor trailer for Bieter's Transfer the pay was double what I would earn driving for Joe Beers. So when Bieter's would call me I would drive for them and the other days I drove for Joe Beers. About a month or so of driving for two companies, Bieter's told me that Evans Delivery in Allentown was looking for a tractor trailer driver. They wrote a letter to Evans Delivery and gave me a strong recommendation. Evans Delivery hired me and I quit driving for Bieter's and Joe Beers. About this time I was introduced by a businessman friend of mine to the Vice President of 1st National Bank of Pen Argyl, PA. I made application for a mortgage with that bank and because I had a full-time job that had excellent pay I qualified for a mortgage.

During all this time we were still living in Belvidere in the parsonage. Conference time was around the corner and I was reminded by the Church Extension Director that I was expected to vacate the parsonage by Conference time because the new Pastor would be moving in. John Frenzi was a big help. He was a licensed real-estate agent in Easton and a very caring man. The mortgage was in review but we needed to move out of the parsonage. John arranged for us to move into a house that he had listed. We were able to rent it on a month-to-month basis until the mortgage was approved and we moved into our new home.

The day finally came and we moved into our new home at Apple Blossom Road and George Streets in Easton, PA. I drove for Evans Delivery for about a year. It was a tumultuous year at that. The truck broke down one night after taking a full trailer from Allentown terminal to the Pottsville terminal. I had already worked a full day and was taking this trailer to Pottsville to exchange for an empty one we needed in Allentown for the next day. It was about 9:00 pm and on Rt. 78 near Hamburg when the transmission failed. I was able to get the rig over to the shoulder and put out the markers. I walked to the next intersection and found a gas station. It was closed but there was a pay phone outside. I called to Pottsville to report the problem. Between the

80

cuss words I was told to leave the truck and get home the best way I knew how. I hitchhiked home.

My truck was an old Reo gas engine with an 8-speed road ranger transmission. It was very slow with very little power. My route was New Jersey. I started in Phillipsburg usually at Ingersoll Rand, where I usually had to wait to be unloaded because the unloading crew was either on break or it was lunch time. There were times when in order to save time I unloaded the material myself.

My last stop was Dairy Pack in Morristown, NJ. There I picked up 40,000 pounds of waxed cartons. Needless to say, it was a long trip home to Allentown because of the inability to get any speed out of the truck.

One day I came to work and my truck had been switched during the night with an older model Reo. The tires were bald and I couldn't lock the trailer pin into the fifth wheel on the tractor. I called the home office in Pottsville and again had to endure a barrage of cuss words. I was told to use my fingers and move the greasy teeth of the fifth wheel until they lined up to enable me to lock the trailer pin. This was enough for me. I told them I resented being cursed at and using the Lord's name as they did. I also refused to take the chance of trying to lock the fifth wheel as they described. Besides the tires were not road worthy. As the driver I was responsible for any accident that these things could cause. The only action left for me to do was to call the union hall and report the situation.

Within a short time two representatives came driving in with a big black 1964 Bonneville Pontiac. They took one look at the tractor, went into the office, talked with the manager and called the office in Pottsville. If I heard cursing from Pottsville it was nothing compared to what the union representative said to the Pottsville terminal manager.

The union representative told the Pottsville manager that he had to get a better tractor down to Allentown in a certain period of time or he would red tag the company and no one could deliver any freight out of the Allentown branch. I was to be paid while I was waiting for another tractor.

Perhaps the most annoying situation was when we received our weekly pay. I would be paid on Friday morning before I began my run. If I waited to cash the check after I returned from my run or try to cash it Saturday morning, I usually was told at the bank that there were insufficient funds. So after this occurred on several occasions I decided to cash my check on Friday morning on my way to deliver my run.

Our first home, 500
Apple Blossom Rd,
Easton, PA

# Teaching School

During this same year, 1964-1965 w,hile driving for Evans Delivery, I tried to move a very heavy large steel piston for a bulldozer from the trailer to the loading dock. In so doing I strained my back so that I could hardly walk or straighten up. I was off from work and had several doctor visits to a specialist. While in this situation Elaine reminded me that while we lived in Belvidere I had befriended the Superintendent of Warren County schools. Every morning I would leave my office and go to the post office around 10:00 am, check the mail and stop next door at a coffee shop. It was there that I met Mr. Alan Tomlinson, superintendent of Warren County Schools. He told me that there was a need for elementary school teachers and wondered if I ever thought about being a teacher. I dismissed it and knew I was doing what the Lord had called me to do. Now that I was flat on my back lying on the floor to get some relief, I listened to what Elaine was saying and decided to call Mr. Tomlinson to set up an interview. He told me to bring my college transcript along with me. During the interview he checked over my degree and told me that I would qualify for a provisional teaching certificate and would need only a few more courses to be eligible for a permanent certificate. At the same meeting he arranged for me to be interviewed for a position at Mansfield Elementary School located a few miles east of Washington, NJ.

I took the interview and was hired to teach 4th grade language arts and some math. I was able to return to driving for Evans but only a few weeks after the interview, when I returned to the terminal from Morristown, NJ, I was informed that the Allentown terminal was closing. We would have to work out of the Pottsville Terminal. There were three drivers at the Allentown terminal and all three of us refused to drive to Pottsville every day and drive our routes. It was now the beginning of July in 1965 and my intention was to inform the terminal manager the beginning of August that I would be leaving to teach school. Now I found myself out of a job. In order for me to drive for Evans I had to belong to the Teamster Union #773. The union office was in Allentown. I went to the union hall and told them that I was scheduled to start teaching in September but wanted to work the rest of the summer. They suggested that I contact Dick Miers who leased 50 tractors to Matlack Cement Division in Northampton, PA.

The next day I went to see Dick Miers and he said he would hire me to drive the cement tankers if I passed the requirements. There was a written test, a driving test around the yard, backing up and parking. Next was a road test with another driver. I was scheduled to drive with Ted Williams from Northampton to Wilmington, Delaware and unload a tanker under his supervision. Before the trip I had to read the manual on how to properly unload a tanker of powdered cement.

On the assigned day I met Ted. The arrangement was that he would drive to Wilmington and show me how to pressurize the tank and unload the cement. I would drive back. After the run he would report to Dick Miers and tell him if I passed or failed. I passed and was told to call in every night at 7:00 pm to see if I had a trip the next day. Since I was the low man on the roster I seldom had a run on Mondays. However, I would go, report in and sit in the driver's room waiting for a run. There were several times that I was called to deliver what they call a "hot load." It was an order of cement that was to be delivered right away. Other times they used me to return repaired tankers and trailers to the surrounding cement plants. I was even assigned my own truck.

When I was ready to make my run I would arrive early to check out the lights and turn signals and make sure I had the proper paper work for the destination of delivery. If I had a flatbed trailer that was loaded with 520 bags of cement weighing 92 pounds apiece, I always would run my hand under the tarp to feel for skids. If there were skids that meant that a fork lift truck would unload the trailer. No skids meant it would be unloaded by hand. Hopefully there would be some help to unload but many times you unloaded the trailer yourself. The company allowed a sufficient amount of time to unload but if additional time was needed, the customer had to sign a special form and you were paid extra.

Just prior to signing a contract to teach 4th grade I was asked to preach at Vroom Street Evangelical Free Church in Jersey City, NJ. I accepted the opportunity and Elaine I went there for the services. A short time later they called again for us to speak. They were without a Pastor and I had been recommended as a possible candidate. After the second time there the elders asked me to be a candidate. They offered us a very reasonable salary. We told them that we would have to pray about this invitation since I had already signed a contract to teach school. Once again they asked us to return to preach. This time the elders told us the people wanted us to go through the process as a candidate. They said that they thought we were not considering their invitation because we didn't want to raise our children in the city. So they proposed that if we would become their Pastor they would sell the parsonage in Jersey City and build or buy us a home of our choice in Secaucus or Teaneck or another smaller city closer to the church. We left them with a promise that we would definitely pray about their invitation. Elaine and I did that and we could not find peace to make that decision and so we informed them of our decision. I believe that this was in early August of 1965.

A few weeks after our decision we were contacted by the Deacons of First Baptist Church of Philipsburg, NJ to become their interim Pastor. I met with the Deacons and consented to be their interim Pastor beginning the first Sunday in October. They offered us the parsonage and a salary of $35.00 a week. Since we were buying our own home we didn't need the parsonage.

In September 1965 I began teaching 4th grade at Mansfield Elementary school just outside Washington, NJ. I enrolled at the Trenton State College Extension located in Washington, N.J. and began to take the necessary courses required for a permanent Elementary Teachers Certificate. By taking one course each semester I received the permanent teacher's certificate April 1970.

When I resigned the church in Belvidere, the conference sent John Herb to succeed me. About a year into his ministry the church was finally built. They used the blueprints that we had developed with

85

Dominic Lentini. I found out about the completed building long after it was dedicated. I felt a little disappointed that I was not invited to join in with the dedication service. John Herb's ministry lasted for another year when he was moved to another church in the Conference and Pastor Bill Bartron was assigned to replace John Herb. Pastor Bartron began his ministry in Belvidere after the Annual Conference concluded. The sad part with the Belvedere Church is that under Pastor Bartron's ministry the church declined to the point where the Conference decided to close the church. Later in my story I will pick up from here and tell you what happened to Belvidere Bible Fellowship Church.

It was October 1965 when I became the interim Pastor at First Baptist Church on Main Street in Philipsburg, NJ. The month before that I began teaching 4th grade at Mansfield Township Elementary school just east of Washington, NJ.

This turn of events was quite interesting to say the least. The day I met the Principal of Mansfield Elementary school, Mrs. Geraldine Nicholson, it was a real shocker. She had served in the army as a Sergeant and her greeting to me told the story. On her desk was a pile of books that I soon learned were the textbooks I would be using. She told me in quite an authoritative voice that I was required by state law to teach 30 minutes of Phys. Ed. every day and what I did with these text books was up to me. That was all there was to our meeting. I guess you would say it was kind of short and sweet.

I reviewed the textbooks and, with the help of my friend Will Everett who was the other 4th grade teacher, I set up my curriculum.

Will had moved to Belvidere shortly after we arrived to begin the church in the Goodwill Firehouse. He, Judith and their children soon began to attend the services. I also learned that he had been in the pastorate but, for reasons unknown to me, he resigned and began teaching 4th grade at Mansfield Elementary School. Teaching side by side caused us to develop a lasting friendship which continues to this day. After Will left teaching at Mansfield he and his family moved to

Weedsville, NY, where he became the Pastor of the local Baptist Church. We lost contact in the years that followed until Bob and Betty Lutz moved next to us here in Macungie. It was in one of our conversations that I learned that Bob and Will grew up together in Baptistown, NJ, not too far from Flemington. Since there was this connection and neither Bob nor I had seen Will in many years, we decided to drive to Weedsville and visit with him. What a visit we had. We spent several hours reminiscing before we had to leave to return home.

I continued to drive for Matlack Cement on Friday nights and sometimes on a Saturday during the months of September and part of October. The cement season was drawing to an end of the construction season. Around Easter I would again begin driving on Friday evenings and Saturday mornings. When the school year ended I would drive full-time once again for the summer months. I continued with this schedule for another five years. However several times during these five years I was called upon to take a run for Bieter's Transfer located in Alpha, NJ. This usually occurred during the winter months. The regular driver for their Friday night run to their main terminal in Connecticut would request a night off. When this happened they would call me to take his place. This would mean that after teaching for the day, coming home and having supper with the family, I would drive to Alpha about 7:00 pm and pick up a partially loaded trailer.

My next stop was Netcong, NJ to pick up some additional freight to take to their main terminal in Hartford, Connecticut. After arriving at the terminal I would drop this trailer and hook up to another for a return trip. Sometimes I had a full load to be delivered to their other terminal in Trenton, NJ. Other times I dropped a loaded trailer in a large freight yard in New York City. Next I would hook up another trailer and take that to Trenton, NJ. From Trenton I pulled another trailer back to Alpha, NJ. By this time it was just a little past breakfast time. Many times I arrived home just as everyone was getting up. We would have breakfast together. When I returned home I needed to make a decision. Either I would take a quick nap, complete my sermon if not completed for the next day, or if someone was in the hospital I would shower, shave and dress accordingly for the visit. I only made about five or six of these trips.

I will always remember a trip that I was asked to take on one of those Friday nights. It was in the dead of winter and I am not sure if it was January or February. All I know is that it was cold with several inches of snow on the ground.

I left the Alpha terminal as usual and drove to Netcong to load a few pieces of freight. No problems driving to Hartford. Now the trouble started. First of all, the trailer I needed to hook up to had frozen brakes. Normally the driver takes the time to go to the back of the trailer and underneath the back doors is an air tank that controls the air to the trailer brakes. When he had completed his trip in the winter months he was to drain the moisture out of the tank that collects on cold days. Somebody forgot to bleed the tank and the moisture inside the tank was frozen hindering the ability to release the trailer brakes. I went immediately to the garage for help. That was an impossible request. The excuses I got were unbelievable. So I asked for a flare and got under the back of the trailer, ignited the flare and thawed out the tank. Now I could bleed the tank of moisture successfully and release the trailer brakes. Great! I was now ready to head for Trenton and then home.

Driving down the Connecticut Turnpike I looked in my mirrors and saw that I didn't have any trailer lights. The trailer lights and turn signals were working properly when I left the terminal. This was trouble. I surely didn't want to be pulled over by a State Trooper and fined. I was rapidly approaching a rest area and decided to exit there. I began to try to determine where the problem was. Sometimes the main plug from the tractor to the trailer is faulty or not connected properly. The plug checked out. Next I checked the main fuse box in the tractor. This wasn't a problem because right in the middle of the dashboard is the location for the fuses. The protective panel was missing and all the fuses were easily visible. There indeed was a fuse burnt out. No extra fuses were discovered in the cab of the truck. The next thing to do is to call back to the main terminal in Hartford. It was unbelievable to hear the swear words and excuses why they couldn't send someone to me and correct the problem. I was told I was on my own and do the best I can. Well, that wasn't very comforting. There were several inches of snow on the ground and it was very cold. As I stepped out of the phone booth, lying on the snow near my feet was an old-fashioned chewing gum wrapper. This was the kind that had a thin sheet of silver paper attached to the protective layer that covered the stick of gum. Here was my answer. I took the gum wrapper and peeled off the silver paper layer and went back to the cab of the truck. I located the burned-out fuse, wrapped the silver around the fuse and inserted it back into the holder. The trailer lights came on and I pulled out onto the Turnpike. I thanked the Lord for His guidance because I always prayed before I would climb into the cab and start the engine. Since I accepted Christ as my Saviour and committed my life to Him I can confidently count on Him to direct my every step.

Things were going smoothly despite the age and condition of the tractor until I was going across the George Washington Bridge at about 3:00 am. Suddenly the truck brakes locked up and I came to a sudden stop. I couldn't release the trailer brakes. I turned on the four-way flashers and inspected the tractor and trailer to see if there was anything that caught my eye. When I reached the back of the trailer I saw the air tank that holds the built-up air which in turn controls the function of the trailer brakes hanging down on a 45-degree angle. One of the air lines had completely broken off. The only thing holding the tank from falling off completely was the other attached end of the air line connected to the tank. When the pressure drops to an established low pressure, the brakes automatically lock. The tractor has a mechanism that produces a buzzing sound when the air pressure drops to the low danger point. Evidently this mechanism was not in working order because the buzzer never sounded. After finding the problem I climbed back into the cab, disconnected the air flow to the trailer thus releasing the trailer brakes. This meant that the only brakes that I would have to complete the trip were the tractor brakes on the drive wheels. This wasn't so bad because the trailer was empty.

I made it safely across the George Washington Bridge when it began to rain. Slick roads with only the tractor brakes could certainly pose a problem. It would certainly be a tricky ride home. But the problems on this run were not over yet and neither was I near home. Since it began to rain, I turned on the windshield wipers, they made two passes across the windshield then quit. I prayed for safety before I left the terminal in Alpha, NJ hours before and I admit I started to pray again. I felt calm and watched my speed carefully. All the way back to the terminal in Trenton, N.J. the rain fell but not heavily and I could see fairly well. It was early Saturday morning and the traffic was thin. Even the oncoming traffic with their headlights wasn't a bother and the glare bouncing off the wet roadway was minimal. Soon I pulled into the main terminal in Trenton. I dropped the trailer and reported the problem. I was given the number of the trailer I needed to pull back to the terminal in Alpha. The final log of my trip was uneventful because it had stopped raining. I was relieved when I backed the trailer into the dock and turned off the engine. I filled out the required paper work. I also reported the burnt-out fuse and the windshield wiper problem and dropped them into the designated box. I got into my car, thanked the Lord for a safe trip back to Alpha and in a few minutes I was home safe and sound. Believe it or not, that was the last trip I made for Beiter's Transfer out of Alpha, NJ.

I continued teaching at Mansfield when I heard of an opening at Pohatcong Elementary school. They were looking for a teacher for 6th grade language arts and math. Pohatcong Township School was much closer to my home so I requested an interview. I met with Mr. Mike Frenzi who served as principal. A few days later Mrs. Geraldine Nicholson, the principal of Mansfield Elementary school, called me into her office. She informed me that she was sorry to hear that I was thinking of leaving Mansfield and said that Mr. Frenzi requested the opportunity to sit in on my class to observe me teaching. I explained to Mrs. Nicholson that because of serving as interim Pastor and some of the growing responsibilities at the church, I was thinking of moving closer to my home and church.

Mr. Frenzi offered me the teaching position. Next, I had an interview with the Warren Glenn school board. Since I was the Pastor of First Baptist Church, did I think there might be a conflict if I began teaching at Pohatcong Elementary School the following September. Mr. Frenzi said we could work that out later if necessary. Working with Mike Frenzi and the other teachers was indeed quite enjoyable. At the end of my first year one of my students entered my name in a contest sponsored by a local radio station for teacher of the week award. I won the prize and was rewarded with a bushel basket filled with shiny red apples.

First Baptist Church, Phillipsburg, NJ

Ladies Trio: Lois, Elaine and Angie

92

Teaching 4<sup>th</sup> grade, Mansfield Elementary

# Building a Church

I continued the schedule of pastoring, teaching and driving for Matlack Cement for about five years. Near the end of the fourth year the church had grown to the size that we needed to consider what our next step would be. The church was full and we began to use the parsonage for additional Sunday school space. On the first floor there was a small room to one side that we used for the baby nursery. We connected speaker wires from the auditorium to the nursery so the people in charge could hear the entire church service. The primary department was on the second floor. The men of the church formed a work crew and we paneled the walls of the basement for the youth department.

I began to talk with the Deacons about the need to think about acquiring land to relocate the church. They didn't object, neither were they overly excited. The year was about 1968 or 1969. Finances were tight and the economy was questionable at least in the eyes of some of the people. One elderly couple said to me as I visited with them and we talked about the need to build, that it couldn't be done because the people only give nickels and dimes.

Soon after talking with the Deacons I was on my way to Harmony to the print shop to pick up an order that was ready. Driving down Belvidere toward Harmony I noticed a sign that 7 ½ acres was for sale. I saw the sign but thought nothing of it. On the way home from the printer I passed the sign again. All the way home I couldn't get that sign out of my mind. As soon as I got home I told Elaine that I needed to clean up, change my clothes and drive back over to inquire about the land that was for sale. Before I left home I prayed for God's will. I am sure I prayed a few short prayers as I drove over to check on the property that was for sale.

I went back to Belvidere road and drove into the drive along side of the for sale sign. I parked the car and made my way to the front door. I took a deep breath and knocked. The door opened and an elderly man

94

greeted me. I identified myself and stated my reason for knocking on his door. He invited me in.

Our conversation lasted for a considerable amount of time. I learned that he was a believer and that he was asking $20,000.00 for the land. The entrance into the large part of the land was only 30 feet wide. The accepted width for a road needed to be 40 feet. He would give an extra 10 feet from his property so that the township couldn't turn down the construction of the church. He also added that he would accept a down payment of $5,000.00 and he would carry the balance with no interest. He also added that we didn't have to make any payments for a full year. He was only interested and anxious to have a church built on the property. His name was Clarence Smith and he was a brother to Dorothy Griffin, a member of the church. Before I left Mrs. Smith offered me a cup of coffee and a piece of freshly baked apple pie. I left their home thanking the Lord for what had already been discussed.

I called the Deacons together for a meeting and presented the proposition to them. I wish I could say they were as excited as I was but they listened carefully. I persuaded them to accompany me to visit with the Smiths and have him review the agreement that he had presented to me. When I mentioned that Mrs. Smith had baked a wonderful apple pie, I believe that clenched their decision. I made the phone call and set up the meeting with the Smiths.

I first needed to think how we were going to raise the down payment money. We only had $1,000.00 in the building fund. Over the years as pastor of the church I had made friends with the president of the bank where the church had done business for many, many years. It was only about a year and half ago that the bank had loaned us the needed funds to have a new roof put on the church. We still had a small balance remaining on that note.

After setting up the appointment with the president of the bank I found myself sitting in his office. After some cordial remarks I got down to business. I explained why I had asked to see him and the opportunity to purchase the land. He was quite interested in the idea and said that he would loan the church the money and add the $5,000.00 to the remaining balance of our original loan. You can imagine how elated I was when I left the bank.

The next step was to notify the Deacons about my visit to the bank. When we all met together I explained the conversation I had with the bank president. After a few minutes of discussion the Deacons agreed to call a congregational meeting to present the proposal to the church. The date was set and the announcement appeared in the church bulletin. That special congregational meeting was also announced from the pulpit as described in the church's constitution and by-laws.

The night of the meeting we had a good turnout. Questions were asked and answered. There was a wonderful spirit and the atmosphere was God honoring. A motion was introduced to proceed with the proposal. The vote was taken and passed with one abstention. It is to be noted that a short time later that individual apologized and said he was wrong. That same individual later became very involved in the construction of the church building.

The next day I met with the bank president and the papers were prepared. All we needed to do now was to have the church officers sign the documents. The officers eagerly signed the papers and the down payment was given to Mr. Clarence Smith.

Mr. Smith had the land surveyed and found out that it wasn't 7 1/2 acres but 8 3/4 acres. Mr. Smith informed me of the results of the survey and said he wouldn't change the price or our agreement. Shortly after talking with Mr. Smith, Mr. Murphy called me. Mr. Murphy was a neighbor to the Smiths. He told me that he found out that we purchased Mr. Smith's field which joined an acre of his property. He further said that several building contractors had contacted him and Mr. Smith to purchase their properties to build a road and several houses on the property. Mr. Smith's land fronted on Belvidere Rd., and Mr. Murphy's fronted on Red School Lane. Mr. Murphy continued to say that he was very pleased that we had purchased Mr. Smith's land to build a church. He had an acre that neither he nor any member of his family wanted so he was willing to sell the acre to us for $1.00. Now we had just a few feet short of 10 acres to build on.

A building committee was established with the plan to visit other recently built churches to select a style that would meet our needs. We toured Clinton Baptist Church and drove to Batavia, NY to see their new building. They both were designed and built by a company specializing in church buildings. The trip to Batavia was quite a trip. Ed and Helen Dickey drove their car with Paul and Beverly Heller as passengers. Elaine and I drove our car with Jim and Goldie Alexander as passengers. We left Phillipsburg very early on a Saturday morning arriving at Batavia, New York around noon. We spent about an hour or so touring the church building and speaking with the pastor.

On the way home we spotted an old Railroad Station that had been converted into a restaurant. We entered the station which served as a reception area. Along the walls were small box-like compartments that held railroad tickets. The tickets turned out to be items on the menu. You selected your entrée and were escorted to your seat in a reconditioned railroad car. When the waiter asked for your order you handed him the ticket. He looked it over and punched it as if you were riding on to your destination. After enjoying a wonderful meal and time of fellowship we started for home. It was a long ride home. Actually we arrived home about midnight. That was Saturday so getting up early for church services the next day was a little struggle.

In the year that followed we concentrated on paying off the bank loan. A sketch of the new church property was mounted on the inside of the front door of the old church building. As funds came into the building fund the sketch was colored green to indicate what amount of the land was paid for. We were not in a hurry to begin to consider the next step in the church's construction. I was still teaching 6th grade at Warren Glenn Elementary School and driving tractor trailer for Matlack Cement Division in the summer months. I had only been at First Baptist for a little over three years and already we had filled the church with over 100 regular worshippers.

One day I was contacted by E. L. Jarman who was developing a church building organization. He was in the process of building a church in Brick, NJ and had heard that we were planning to build a church building sometime in the future. In our meeting he discussed what his company could do as far as providing for us a complete building including pews, baptistery, carpeting, etc. He quoted a price of $150,000 turnkey with ample Sunday school space and an auditorium that would seat over 300 people. The building would be in the shape of a cross. The educational section would be 160 ft. across the front of the building and the foyer and auditorium would measure 108 ft. from the front door to the baptistery window. Turnkey meant that the church would be built complete with carpet, pews, heating, air conditioning, and parking lot completed. Our responsibility would be to paint the inside of the building. It all sounded so wonderful. The only major thing standing in our way was the money.

At this time we had accumulated only $1,000.00 in the building fund and the property was not fully paid for. As I discussed this with Mr. Jarman, he continued to tell me of his background with fund-raising. He had many years of experience and had recently completed a large fund-raising campaign with Philadelphia College of Bible in Langhorne, PA. [Over the years since then Philadelphia College of Bible had changed its name to Cairn University.] I asked Mr. Jarman many questions about fund-raising and he graciously answered them all. He had the knowledge and background to establish a bond program with a local bank. The bonds would be printed with the name of the church as the issuer and the name of the bank as the payee. The amount of interest to be paid was set at 8%. The bonds ranged from $250 up to $5,000. I believe the breakdown was as follows: $250, $500, $1,000, $2,000, $2,500, and $5,000.

After this first meeting with Mr. Jarman, I called a special meeting with the Deacons to report to them about my meeting with Mr. Jarman. After discussing what I had learned from Mr. Jarman, the Deacons agreed to have a meeting with Mr. Jarman to review what he had told me.

The meeting was arranged with Mr. Jarman and the full Deacon Board. Mr. Jarman was in the area building a church in Bricktown, NJ. Many questions were raised by members of the Deacon Board and fully answered by Mr. Jarman. After we excused Mr. Jarman the Deacon Board voted unanimously to have Mr. Jarman return and address the congregation at a special meeting called for that purpose.

A date was agreed upon and the meeting was well attended. Mr. Jarman presented the bond program to the congregation. He also introduced the church layout that he had previously presented to me and the Deacons. After a period of questions and answers Mr. Jarman was excused from the meeting. The meeting continued with the Deacons and the members of the congregation discussing the proposed bond program and church construction. There was some apprehension on the part of some of the people since I still was a part-time pastor, the economy was in question at this time and this would take a big step of faith. In fact I had only been their pastor for three years. It was true that we had seen a considerable increase in attendance over this time and we had in fact almost filled the old church facilities to capacity. However, a motion was made, seconded and passed with one negative vote that we precede with Mr. Jarman and the construction of the church.

During the next several months the bonds were printed and ready to be purchased. I was elected to oversee the purchase of the bonds and the keeping of the records. The congregation purchased about one half of the issue. It was a good investment because the bonds would yield 8% interest payable at the duration of the bond issue. I began approaching others outside the church and sold the remaining half of the issue. As the bonds were sold the money was deposited into the construction account.

While all this activity was happening I continued to teach at the Warren Glenn Elementary School as the remedial reading teacher, teaching half-day sessions, Tuesdays through Friday.

Mr. Jarman was a pilot and flew his own twin engine plane. He arranged to fly Ed Savacool, Paul Heller and me to McDonough, New York to tour Ford Homes. McDonough, NY, a quaint country village, was a short distance from Cortland, NY. The company has built pre-engineered homes for many years. They also began expanding their business to building church buildings. We watched them construct sections for a home that had been ordered. The construction consisted of 4' by 8' sections complete with exterior plywood, insulation, electrical connections and interior drywall. These sections were loaded onto flatbed trailers and covered with tarps ready to be delivered after the last section was loaded onto the trailer. The company was highly rated for the quality of construction that went into their buildings. We enjoyed meeting the management and crew of Ford Homes as well as the flight.

While the bonds were being printed and sold a building committee was formed. The committee consisted of Ed Dickey, Ed Savacool, Paul Heller, Jim Alexander, Cliff Stott, Tony DiVietro and me. At this point in the process a congregational meeting was called to vote to proceed with the building plans. I mentioned that when the vote was taken we had one negative vote. That negative vote was Tony DiVietro. However sometime after the congregational meeting when he cast his negative vote, he asked me if he could address the church at one of our services. When he addressed the congregation he was very humble and sincere. He said after thinking about the need to step out in faith and construct the church building, he realized that he was wrong to vote the way he did. He remembered another building program in which he had been involved previously that had many problems and he was reliving those days when he cast his vote. He was sorry and told the congregation that he was wrong to feel that way and asked them to forgive him for his actions. The congregation graciously forgave him and from that time forward, Tony became very much involved when the actual construction began.

We still owed Mr. Smith for the balance of the price of the land. Mr. Smith insisted that we pay him later and that we should proceed in getting the church built. So all the documents were drawn up and properly signed so that we could proceed with ordering the building from Ford Homes. A ground-breaking service was announced to take place on a Sunday Afternoon. The Friday before the actual ground-breaking service would be held, the excavator was free to begin excavating. Sunday afternoon we conducted the ground-breaking service as planned. All the officers from all the ministries of the church were present to turn over a spade of dirt even though the ground had already been broken by the excavator the Friday before.

After the ground-breaking service, I walked Mrs. Elsie Allen up to the place where the excavator had already begun to remove some ground. Earlier in the days when we first began talking about building a new church to replace the old building on South Main Street, Elsie and her husband Ed had remarked one day when I visited with them in their home that the church would never be built because the people were poor givers. When Mrs. Allen saw how much earth had been removed she turned to me and said: "I believe you are going to do it."

The construction actually had begun. Mr. Jarman became the contractor and would be on the job Monday through Friday. He flew his plane from Illinois to ABE and rented a car for the week. He roomed at the Holiday Inn near Allentown and commuted to the job site every day. A construction trailer was erected at the job site and served as Mr. Jarmon's office. I completed the school year teaching remedial reading and moved from part-time pastor to full-time. Things were moving along quite well.

Mr. Jarman had hired two men experienced in putting up the forms for the basement walls and constructing the footers. He received an excellent price for cement from Steckel Concrete Company in Phillipsburg. The only problem with the concrete men he hired was that they did not have a good reputation. This meant that they could not arrange to have the concrete forms delivered to the job site on their signature. Mr. Jarman made an agreement with a concrete form company from Philadelphia but we would have to pick them up ourselves. Mr. Jarman asked me if I could arrange to truck these forms from Philadelphia to the church site. I spoke with Speedy Griffin and he allowed me to take a tractor and a 40-ft. trailer to Philadelphia to pick up the concrete forms. I remember this very clearly. Tom Allen rode along with me. It was a dark, rainy, dismal, cold December day. For some unknown reason to me I couldn't get the heater to work and we were chilled to the bone by the time we arrived at the concrete form company.

We were greeted by the biggest black man I had ever seen in my life. He wasn't too happy to see us and told us so by talking about going out in the cold damp rain, etc. I asked him where their supply yard was located. He responded that it was several blocks down that same street. I then asked him if there was a coffee shop near their supply yard to which he answered in the affirmative. I told him that we would drive to the yard and on the way pick up some coffee and donuts for his men and ourselves and together we would load the trailer with the concrete forms. This was a union shop and I knew the way the workers dealt with others helping them on a job. But the offer of the coffee and doughnuts hit the spot with him and his crew. We followed through with our promise and they with theirs so that in a short time we had all the concrete forms loaded into the trailer and we were on our way home.

The work on the foundation was going very slowly. Again the men that Jarman hired to do the foundation and form the walls were quite slow. This was important because Ford Homes was constructing the building in sections. When a section was completed it was loaded onto a flatbed trailer and covered to protect it from the weather. Ford Homes did not have a warehouse to store the completed sections so they were loaded onto flatbed trailers until the building was completed. Ford Homes was building the sections faster than the concrete men were doing the foundation work. While the foundation was being constructed a union block layer company put up pickets because we did not hire union workers. The slowness of the foundation work became critical because Ford Homes had given Mr. Jarman a date when they would deliver the building to our site and they would have a team of men with them to construct the building connecting all the sections that had been pre-engineered by them. A decision had to be made. Only half of the basement wall had been completed. Mr. Jarman contacted the union block layer company that had picketed us and made an arrangement that they would complete the other half of the foundation with cement blocks so that the foundation walls were ready when Ford Homes delivered the sections.

The day finally came. The foundation walls were completed and 18 tractor trailer loads of building sections arrived at the church site. It took the Ford Homes construction crew five days to put the entire building together. Next was the completion of the roof shingles and exterior siding. In deciding what exterior siding we would prefer, Mr. Jarman suggested that some of the committee drive to Bricktown, NJ where he was in the process of completing another Ford Homes built church. This church was much smaller than the one we were constructing. It was at Bricktown that I met the Pastor, Dick Fisher. He introduced me to the Foreman on that job by the name of Jerry Elliott. In talking with Pastor Fisher and Jerry Elliott we got an ear full.

Mr. Jarman was doing things to cut costs to keep it within his quote but doing substandard work. Later we met with Mr. Jarman and discussed with him some of the problems we had heard about from Pastor Fisher. He acknowledged them and said he was not attempting these things on our job. However, we already had worked out a problem with him when our building was being constructed by the Ford Homes crew.

The steel beams that served to give us an open span for the fellowship hall were inadequate to support the floor system and the walls and roof were not even in place. He agreed to correct the problem by welding another beam to the existing beams. Doug Mace, the Lopatcong Township engineer and a member of the church supervised the procedure to ensure that the steel would in fact support the structure.

In our meeting with Mr. Jarman to discuss how the steel situation would be resolved, we learned that the only building he ever supervised was building a garage. The church in Bricktown was the first church he supervised and ours was the second. Soon after he began our construction he contracted with the Washington New Jersey Assemblies of God to build a church there as well. It wasn't long until we were contacted by the Washington Assemblies Pastor to discuss with us the problems they were having with Mr. Jarman. In fact shortly after meeting with the Assemblies Pastor he informed us that they dismissed Mr. Jarman and voted to complete the church themselves.

Doug Mace and I arranged to have a meeting with Mr. Jarman to discuss the issues that we were having with his inability to properly oversee the construction as well as the difficulties he had with the churches at Bricktown and Washington. He acknowledged that there were some issues but that he endeavored to do what was right for the remainder of our construction. The project moved along with Mr. Jarman as contractor. Jerry Elliott and his family began attending our church much to the dismay of Mr. Jarman. In fact he personally informed Jerry that he would appreciate it if Jerry and his family no longer attended our church or befriended us. Jerry was the foreman of the Bricktown and Washington church construction but since the churches had dismissed Mr. Jarman, Jerry was no longer his employee. Jerry and his family continued to attend faithfully until they went to New Guinea as missionaries.

The construction of our church continued with the completion of the interior. The sanctuary was completed first because the pews were scheduled to be delivered and installed. The carpet had been delivered which was included in the price of the building but now needed to be installed. Bruce and Jerri Watson were members of the church and her father sold and installed carpet. He volunteered to lay the carpet free of charge if he could have volunteers to assist him. Several men assisted him in the installation of the carpet. The auditorium looked wonderful with the carpet installed. The pews would be arriving shortly to add the final touch to the sanctuary.

As the construction moved closer to completion it became evident that the funds raised with the sale of the bonds was insufficient to complete the construction. It was estimated that we were $100,000.00 short of estimated costs to complete the project. This was brought to our attention by Mr. Jarman. He suggested that we issue a second series of bonds. Another congregational meeting convened and after the discussion of the matter it was decided that we would take a special offering to raise some money for the deficit. After the special offering was received we had received $50,000.00, half the amount needed. A second series of bonds for $50,000.00 were sold and funds were in line with what the anticipated cost would be.

With the steady growth of the church and the increase of my pastoral duties I talked with Mr. Frenzi about the church duties and that I would not be returning the following year to teach. The timing was just right because the 6th grade teacher that I had replaced wanted to return to the classroom again. She had taken the position of a part-time remedial reading teacher after her child was born and now that her child was starting first grade she wanted to return to teaching again. This became an ideal setup because she could return to teaching 6th grade and I would be the part-time remedial reading teacher. I would take this position for the next two years.

I was completing my final weeks as the part-time remedial reading teacher at Warren Glenn, and would always stop at the church on the way home to see if I could be of any assistance with the work crew. As I entered the building one of the workers said that Mr. Jarman was there with several men to see the building. This was hard for me to believe because Mr. Jarman, who flew his own airplane from Illinois to ABE airport, had called me over the weekend to say he couldn't fly in because of weather conditions. His procedure was to be on the job during the week and fly home to Illinois on Friday afternoon and fly back to ABE early Monday morning.

As I walked into the sanctuary I could see footprints on the newly laid carpet. Since the educational section and foyer were still being spackled and sanded to get ready for paint, white dust collected on the shoes and was easily tracked into the sanctuary. Needless to say, I was not happy to learn that Mr. Jarman had lied to me. It is difficult to describe the mixed emotions that raced through my mind at that time. The problems he had with the other two churches, the fiasco with the concrete crew and inability of them securing the forms for the basement walls, the wrong size steel to span the fellowship hall along with other small problems during the construction surely meant that we needed to have a serious meeting with Mr. Jarman.

After asking a few questions of the work crew, I was able to locate the church in Maryland where several of the men from that church had been here that morning looking at our building. I made contact with the Pastor from Frederick, Maryland and set up a meeting. I took our cost sheets with me and it was at this meeting that I learned that Mr. Jarman had flown a few men from that church up to see our building. Mr. Jarman had met with them and was in the process of selling them the same building he was building for us. He also quoted the same price as he did for us. However our costs sheets indicated that we were overextended by $100,000.00. After meeting with this pastor I returned home.

Several from our building committee met with Mr. Jarman. We faced him about what he told me about not being able to be on the job but rather flew men from Frederick, Maryland to see the construction of our building with the hopes that he could sell the same building to them. He was not a very happy person, especially when he found out that I had already met with the pastor and shared our costs with him. At the conclusion we unanimously agreed to dismiss Mr. Jarman from being the contractor.

The remainder of oversight of the building was done by members of the building committee working together. A plumbing warehouse in Allentown gave us the all the plastic and copper pipe needed to complete the plumbing. Later they would give us all the baseboard electric heat for the entire building. They also gave us all that we needed to complete all the restrooms in the building. Two years later the same company donated all the equipment for central air conditioning. The men of the church did the installation. The owner of a paint store in Allentown also donated all the paint for the interior.

The Presbyterian Home in Belvidere was sold to the Freeholders of Warren County for additional office space. Jim Alexander, one of the members of the church was driving past the building that was being gutted and saw several old chandeliers on the junk pile in the back of the building. He passed the word on to me and I went to the Freeholders office in Belvidere to see about the chandeliers. The gentleman in charge said he didn't want to go through all the paper work to put the chandeliers out for bid. I told him I was there to ask his permission to take away some of the junk on the junk pile. He smiled and said: "Be my guest." I took the chandeliers back to the church where they were stripped down, sanded and sprayed a gold color. To this day some forty plus years later they are still hanging in the foyer of the church.

Mr. Jarman when he was overseeing the construction of the building thought that we had too much top soil and made arrangements to have it sold and trucked away. Now that he was gone and we were completing the work ourselves, we now needed a considerable amount of top soil for final grading. We would have to deal with this later.

Dick Hummer of Mt. Bethel, PA received the bid to blacktop the driveways and parking lot. I was watching the first truck load of black top being driven into the church lot. I was amazed to see Dick himself driving the first truck load. I inquired about that to the foreman of the blacktop crew and he told me that they were short of drivers. I informed him that I could drive a tractor trailer. Immediately he informed Dick Hummer what I had said. Dick asked me if I wanted to work the next day. It was Friday when Dick came with the first load. I said I would do it and then asked him if he could use another driver. He was delighted and so early Saturday morning Jim Alexander and I started the day delivering blacktop to the church lot. We drove all day and the lot and driveways were completed. To our surprise Dick Hummer drastically reduced his cost for the blacktop.

Dick Hummer was an understanding and softhearted businessman. It was to him that I went back to explain that we were considerably short

107

of top soil for the finished grading around the building. He said if I would drive the truck he would donate all the top soil we needed. I was to come to his yard at quitting time and the foreman would load a huge tri-axle dump truck with top soil. I would drive it to the church lot and dump the load and return the truck back to his yard. I did this four times until we had enough top soil to complete the grading.

To complete the building project a work crew of church members was established. People with different work skills volunteered their time whether during the week or on Saturdays. Elaine and Goldie Alexander organized several women to prepare lunch for those working on Saturday. However after we ate those terrific lunches it was difficult to get them to go back to work.

The day finally came that we received the occupancy permit and were now able to hold the first service in the new building. What a day that was! The people were excited and were praising God that the day finally came for them to worship in the new facility. Prior to the opening day we made plans to be able to transport the people who used to walk to church at the old building to be able to ride to the new church. We purchased an older bus from the Fellowship Church that they weren't using because it had brake problems. I made arrangements to take the bus to Belvidere to Answorth Scott to check out the brakes. Answorth had a fleet of school buses that were contracted out for public school student transportation. Tom Allen agreed to drive the bus to Belvidere and I would follow in my car. I was behind Tom when he came to the first stop sign. It was the stop sign at the end of Third Street that went down a hill to a dead-end onto Belvidere Road. I saw the brake light go on but Tom wasn't slowing down. He went through the stop sign and swerved a sharp right onto Belvidere Road. Eventually he was able to stop as the bus slowed down of its own accord. I stopped behind the bus to talk with Tom. He emerged from the bus as white as a sheet. If another vehicle had been coming up Belvidere Road at the same time as Tom ran through the stop sign, there would have been a terrible accident.

After gaining his composure Tom got back into the bus. He drove slowly and carefully to Answorth Scott's garage in Belvidere. I took Tom back to his home and I returned to mine. A few days later Answorth called me to say all that was needed was the booster chamber. He had one that he installed without charge.

The next day we drove the bus to Jim Alexander's home. Jim's father-in-law had a large garage that we could use to prepare the bus for painting. School buses used by churches could not be yellow; they needed to be painted a different color. We chose brown and white. This was the start of what turned out to be a fleet of five buses all painted alike and used to transport people to Sunday school, church services and youth meetings.

Now that we were worshipping in the new building the next business on the agenda was to sell the old church building and parsonage. It was brought to our attention that a group of black people had joined together to form a church fellowship and might be interested in the old church. Rev. David Moore was their pastor and he was eager to meet with me to discuss the possibility of them purchasing the buildings.

The selling price was set at $35,000.00. Unfortunately Rev. Moore and his small congregation did not have the finances. I went to our bank to inquire if it would be possible for the bank to loan them the money if we were willing to sign on their behalf. This was not acceptable to the bank policy. It seemed that all options were closed to them for purchasing the buildings. One of our members sold some property and told me he would give $5,000.00 to our church and I should lower the selling price by that same amount. After speaking with him for a brief period of time I suggested that he should consider carrying the mortgage at a reasonable amount of interest. He agreed and the congregation of Grace Baptist Church now had a place of their own.

The highlight of all that had gone on before with the erection of the building was the Sunday we dedicated the church. Again the church was filled and we all rejoiced in what the Lord had done for us. It was a day to long remember.

Mr. Jarman taking Ricky for a ride in his airplane

Ground-breaking

Construction

Volunteers

113

Completion!

115

Dedication

# Ministry Growth and Opportunities

The next day of celebrating was the celebrating of our first anniversary. Those present on the platform were: Rev. Bryan Jones, Executive Director of the IFCA, Pastor Hoye, who served as one of the previous pastors and Rev. Russell Allen from the Fellowship Church. It was a day filled with excitement and praise to the Lord for His leading in all of our lives.

Our first Sunday school rally day in the new building was a great success. It had been suggested to me from a dear friend that there was a musical family from Hamburg, PA called the Yoder family that he had used for a special occasion at his church. The Yoder family consisted of Mr. & Mrs. John Yoder, their daughter, their son and his girlfriend. They sang accompanied by several guitars. Their music was done in good taste and our people enjoyed them thoroughly. They also sang a few numbers during the worship service. After the service the Yoders came back to our home for a scrumptious dinner prepared by Elaine. The Yoders talked with us for a few hours before leaving for their home. They told us that the honorarium which was given to them by us and other churches was going to finance their missions trip to the Virgin Islands. They had been invited by the Virgin Island Baptist Missions agency to play and preach at some of the mission churches on the Islands.

It was about a week later after the Yoders had returned to their home that I received a phone call from Mr. Yoder. He said that their family had met to talk about their upcoming trip to the Virgin Islands and wanted me to join them to be the speaker. Mr. Yoder admitted that he would rather sing than speak. If I consented to go with them my travel expenses would all be taken care of. I shared this with Elaine and my Board of Deacons. The Board of Deacons released me and I drove to Hamburg in the early morning hours of a very cold January day. The Yoder family and I were driven to the Philadelphia airport by a member of their church. It was no problem finding reservations to fly to Washington, DC and make the connection to take a plane to Puerto Rico. When we arrived at Washington, DC airport we learned that our flight to Puerto Rico was delayed. We had nothing to do but to walk around and wait. After four hours of waiting I asked the airport attendant at the check-in desk how much longer we would have to wait. We had to make a connection from Puerto Rico to St. Thomas and it was most likely we would miss that connection. I also said that we had been waiting for four hours and we were hungry. The attendant smiled and said she was sorry for the delay and gave me passes to go to a certain room and to help ourselves to some food. The food was delicious and that made our wait more tolerable.

Finally our flight was called for boarding. We arrived in Puerto Rico in record time but we had missed the flight to St. Thomas. We were told they were sorry about our delay in Washington, DC but there would not be another flight to St. Thomas until the next morning. I turned to the attendant and told her our delay was the fault of the airline and not ours so they would have to call a cab, put us up in a hotel and provide meals for all of us. The attendant thought for a minute and said she would see what she could do. In a few minutes she called me over and told me that a small plane was available to fly us all over to St. Thomas. We could board the plane in fifteen minutes. It was a small two engine plane with a pilot and a copilot and seats for all of us with a few extra. It was a short flight but all over water. I remember looking into the open cockpit and watching the rpm gauges for the two engines to make sure they were operating without a problem. The airport hangar was an old, World War II Quonset hut. We were met by the director of the Virgin Islands Baptist Mission agency and brought to his home.

After breakfast the next morning we all went to the Bavonia Baptist Church where the Yoders sang and I preached. I remember calling Elaine after church to tell her we arrived safely and to tell her the temperature was a warm 80 degrees there.

During the next ten days we held church services and street meetings in St. Thomas and St. Croix. We spent several days in St. Croix holding meetings at a small Baptist church. After a church service one evening we were invited to go for a bite to eat with one of the deacons. I was excited about the possibility of trying out some special island food. We drove for a few miles down the winding road blowing the horn at almost every turn in the road. It seems that all the drivers on the island did the same. All you could hear were horns blowing. Finally up ahead beyond the palm trees we saw bright lights. Now perhaps I would have the opportunity to try some island food. My heart sank when we rounded the corner and pulled into a McDonald's. So much for island food.

Before returning to St. Thomas and preparing for our return trip home we spent the next day touring St. John Island. Our trip to the Virgin Islands was coming to an end and we recounted the many experiences we enjoyed together on this trip.

One of the groups that grew quickly was the Youth Group. We planned an outing to use the Victory Valley Camp of the Bible Fellowship Church located in Zionsville. The camp had ample facilities for our group. Several adults volunteered to join us for the day. I suggested that instead of hot dogs and hamburgers I make "Hunters Stew" for everyone. I borrowed a large stainless-steel pot from my mother-in-law. The church would supply several pounds of hamburger and the kids would each bring a peeled potato, carrot and onion. Doug Mace and I would do the rest. While the youth group was busy with games and other activities, Doug and I went to work. We first built a fire and arranged a stand to support the large pot. Next we cut up all the vegetables the group brought. I put a small amount of water into the pot that was heating and slowly added the raw hamburger to cook. As the hamburger cooked I slowly added more water and began to add the chopped-up vegetables. More water was added and the hunters stew began to cook. While it was being prepared a few of the young people came to the fire and wrinkled up their noses and said they wouldn't eat that stew.

The morning slipped away quickly and it was time to serve the hunters stew. One by one they came to fill up their bowls. They were tired from all the games and activities in which they participated and above all else they were hungry. It seemed very strange that even the ones who wrinkled up their noses and said they wouldn't eat any of the stew came back for seconds. It wasn't long and the stew was all gone. In fact, we all enjoyed the stew immensely and there were no complaints. The day turned out to be a great day and everyone expressed their pleasure in enjoying the day.

I had one more project to complete as a result of the outing when I got home. I had to clean up the large cooking pot I had borrowed from my mother-in-law. The bottom was completely covered in black soot from the fire. I scrubbed and scrubbed but to no avail. With my tail between my legs I sheepishly returned the ruined pot to my mother-in-law who, although not very happy with its condition, just gave me her Metzger look that told me exactly what she was thinking, but she never said a word. I got the message. The pot was completely ruined and never again could be used.

Our church attendance increased steadily. In a short period of time the church was filled and plans were made to go to two services on a Sunday morning to accommodate the people.

After a year or two with two services it was decided to enter into another building program to increase the size of the sanctuary. At a congregational meeting the consensus was to extend the sanctuary and add on two side rooms for changing rooms for baptismal services. However we would not consider starting until we had received at least $50,000.00 in the building fund.

Bruce Watson, a member of the church and an architect, was asked to prepare the blueprints for the expansion. While the plans were being drawn up, funds began pouring into the building fund. The people were excited. At this same time one of the older ladies of the church passed away and the church was listed in her will. Still later there was another member who passed away and he listed the church in his will. Before the actual start of the new addition $350,000.00 was in the building fund. Now there was enough in the building fund to complete

120

the new addition and we could go back to one service on a Sunday morning.

It was learned that the Bible Fellowship Church in Belvidere that was designed while I served as pastor was going to be closed. It was only a few years old, but the attendance had dropped to such a low figure that keeping the doors open was next to impossible.

All of the churches in the Bible Fellowship denomination at this time fell under the direction and authority of the Board of Directors of the Bible Fellowship Church. Rev. Jack Hartman was the president of the Board of Directors. I requested a meeting with him to discuss the possibility of First Baptist Church of Phillipsburg securing the building. An agreement was reached between the Board of Directors of the Bible Fellowship Church and our church that we would lease the church in Belvidere for $350.00 a month for three years with an option to purchase. After the three-year lease we would revisit the agreement. I met with the elders of First Baptist to discuss the possibility of entering into this lease with the Bible Fellowship denomination.

It is to be noted that some time before this took place we had a revision of the church constitution and the names of the officers were changed as follows. Deacons became elders and trustees became deacons.

I presented a plan to the elder board that I would drive to Liberty University where Kirk DiVietro was ready to graduate. Kirk was one of our young men who we assisted in moving to Liberty with his wife and family to study for the ministry. The board gave their approval and I followed through with the meeting with Kirk. Originally when Kirk felt the call of the Lord to study for the ministry, I drove him to Liberty University for his initial interview. While in Lynchburg he was able to find part-time employment. I was able to secure with my signature the rental of a trailer off campus for housing, secure fuel and an electrical hook up so that everything would be ready when he would arrive with his family and begin his studies.

121

As I met with Kirk to talk about the plan for Belvidere, he was excited and readily agreed. The plan was that if the people of First Baptist in Phillipsburg would approve the lease agreement with the Bible Fellowship denomination, I would request the people attending First Baptist from Belvidere to agree to be the seed families and help get the church in Belvidere established. Kirk would be installed as the pastor of the Belvidere church and I would serve as his mentor.

I returned from Lynchburg and gave my report to the elders. Next a congregational meeting was called and the plan presented for their consideration and vote. After a time of discussion the vote was taken and unanimously passed.

The church in Belvidere was now called: First Baptist Church of Belvidere, NJ. The agreement (for the purpose of record keeping and legality until Belvidere could be properly incorporated) would be under First Baptist Church of Phillipsburg. The official name would therefore be: First Baptist Church of Phillipsburg, Belvidere Branch.

It was a rewarding experience to assist not only in the forming of Grace Baptist Church of Phillipsburg, NJ but now also First Baptist Church of Belvidere, NJ. For many years on Thanksgiving eve, the congregations of Grace Baptist and First Baptist of Belvidere would join with us for worship and fellowship.

Elaine and I had a wonderful opportunity to tour the Holy Lands after the conclusion of the Yom Kippur War in 1973. Rev. Jim Bates, pastor of Mansfield Baptist Church in Mansfield, NJ, had signed up to take the tour and had invited us to join him. The tour company had a policy that for every seven people who signed up for the tour you would get one person's trip free. I was able to have enough people from First Baptist sign up so that Elaine and I went free. I really didn't know then what a responsibility it was to care for their luggage, passports and make sure we were all together when it came time to board the bus.

It was a grueling trip. The day before we flew out of Kennedy Airport in New York City, we were busy packing and getting Roxann and Ricky set up at grandma's house. Early that same evening we boarded the bus to go to the airport. Next after arriving I had to make sure all the tickets, passports and luggage, and my people were all accounted for. It was dark when we taxied down the runway to begin our long overnight flight, landing first in Amsterdam, Netherlands.

The flight was smooth with no hitches. It was early morning when we arrived in Amsterdam. Once inside the terminal we were notified that we would have an eight-hour layover before we caught our plane to Israel. The airlines had already arranged a bus tour of Amsterdam for our convenience. We boarded a luxurious bus with very comfortable seats. As we rode around the city square we saw a sea of beautiful tulips in full bloom. The driver showed us places of interest and the unusual building styles we had never seen before. The highlight of the bus trip was a ride in a large glass enclosed passenger canal boat. There are many canals around Amsterdam and we were privileged to see many wonderful sights from the boat. It was raining most of our time in Amsterdam but it turned out to be a delightful several hours.

Once again we boarded the bus that took us to the airport and to our plane. It was quite late when we landed at Tel Aviv airport in Israel. Once again armed soldiers were visible. I helped load our entire luggage onto the top of the bus and then made sure everyone was accounted for as we made our way to the hotel in Jerusalem. At the hotel I made sure everyone had their luggage and was assigned a room. It was after midnight when we finally got to bed – feeling quite exhausted.

The next morning after breakfast we toured the Via Delorosa. This was the very street where Jesus walked. We looked at the shops and listened to our tour guide point out places of interest. It was a very interesting day.

The second day after breakfast we again boarded the bus. All were accounted for and we began a trip to Bethlehem. We hadn't traveled far when Elaine told me she wasn't feeling well. I was concerned about her blood pressure and told the tour guide we needed to find a doctor. He stopped the bus and called for a cab. Elaine and I were taken to the nearest doctor's office but when we arrived we were told the doctor was in America. This happened the second time and after that I instructed the driver to take us back our hotel. The cabby said that he wanted to be paid in American money. The cost of the cab ride was $20.00 American dollars. Once inside the hotel the clerk called for the house doctor. He came to our room and checked Elaine's blood pressure, etc. All was in order and his diagnosis was that she was just extremely exhausted and needed to rest.

After the doctor left I went to see if we could get some food in the dining room. The room was empty. Everyone was out on a tour. I found a woman cleaning the bar area and asked if we could get something to eat. She made two cheese sandwiches and I got a bottle of coke. The price was $5.00. We ate our lunch and rested. When the group came back from their day's outing they all wanted to know how Elaine was feeling. After the evening meal some of the ladies from the church came to be with Elaine. I went downtown with a few of the men. To my surprise I was able to buy a large ice cream cone and a large coke for 25 cents. Quite a difference from the two cheese sandwiches we had at lunch.

The doctor's orders were for Elaine to have bed rest for at least three days. Some of our group had brought some magazines with them and they gladly gave them to me to read while I stayed with Elaine. That night Jack Wyrtzen came to our room and had prayer with us. He and a group of others staying in the same hotel had heard about Elaine and came to visit.

Elaine felt stronger and we completed the rest of the tour visiting many Biblical sites. Perhaps the highlight of our stay in The Holy Land was to participate in a communion service at the Garden Tomb, the place where Jesus' body was laid after His crucifixion and where He arose after the third day. It was a very moving service and one that I will never forget.

Soon we were on our way to Athens, Greece. Once again armed soldiers were at the airport. We had a few days to tour Athens and also Corinth. Reliving the days of the Apostle Paul brought shivers up your spine. I took the opportunity to tour the remains of the Acropolis in Athens and stood on Mars Hill as well. Elaine really enjoyed Athens. The weather was wonderful and the food delicious. The food was quite a change from Israel's food. A few blocks from our hotel on Constitution Square I found a gyro shop. What a delicious gyro! In fact it was so good I had several before leaving Athens for home.

With the Yoder family on the Virgin Islands

Bavoni Baptist Church, St. Thomas

Walter Frank, ground breaking for new addition

Amsterdam, Holland

Glass canal boat
ride

Arriving in Jerusalem

Via Dolorosa

127

Garden Tomb

Athens, Greece

Acropolis

Bema Seat in
Corinth

128

# Phillipsburg Christian Academy

After returning home from our Holy Land tour it was back to work on another project. Pastor Russell Allen of the Fellowship Church of Phillipsburg and I had been meeting regularly to discuss the formation of a Christian School. Since I had some experience teaching in a public school my responsibility was to select the curriculum and determine what grades we would be able to offer to interested families.

Elaine and I took many trips to Christian schools in Pennsylvania, New Jersey, South Carolina and Ohio interviewing school principals and asking many questions. After completing this preliminary study I presented to Pastor Allen my suggestions. He was in full agreement. Next we established a school board made up of several men from each of the two churches. There was a retired school teacher who was a member of First Baptist and he was selected to be the school principal and his wife the school secretary. The formation of PCA was announced from both pulpits and in the daily newspaper. Applications began coming into the school office. At the next school board meeting it was established that PCA would offer 1st through 6th grades. 1st through 3rd would be held at First Baptist Church and 4th through 6th at the Fellowship Church. The curriculum was ordered and PCA officially opened in the fall of 1976.

The student body grew steadily year after year but there was a concern about the two church partnerships since there were some lawsuits leveled against Christian schools at this time. A meeting was scheduled with an appropriate lawyer to discuss the ramifications of the two-church sponsorship of PCA. After the meeting the school board unanimously took the lawyer's advice that one church should be the sponsor of PCA. Since the Fellowship Church had the larger classrooms they became the sponsor of PCA. First Baptist Church would include funds in their annual budget to help finance the school and agreed to promote PCA from the pulpit. PCA continued for over 30 years when the Fellowship Church experienced financial difficulties and a decline in church attendance and enrollment of PCA.

PCA was discontinued and students were encouraged to enroll in another Christian school if they were so inclined.

# Further Ministries

In the fall of 1976 I enrolled for further education at Christian Counseling and Education Foundation founded by Dr. Jay Adams. We would meet every Monday during the school year. In the morning there would be two lectures usually given by Dr. Jay Adams and Dr. John Betler. We would break for lunch which was a fast trip to the nearest McDonald's. It was the best we could do in order to be back for the afternoon sessions. In the morning sessions we received instructions to be applied to the Principles of Christian Counseling. In the afternoon we would sit in on two actual counselling sessions. Each of us would have the opportunity to observe Jay Adams in his counselling session and also John Betler with his session.

After these actual counselling sessions were concluded and the parties being counseled left the building, the entire class would assemble together and have the opportunity to review the sessions we had observed with Jay Adams and John Betler. Sometimes they would ask us what we had observed during their session. After we concluded the session we all left to go home. It was a long day.

During my student days at CCEF I made some new friends. One of my new-found friends was a pastor from a large church in Harrisburg. It was during one of our lunch breaks that he asked me many questions about my call to the ministry and the scope of my ministry at that time. I had served as student pastor at Mountain View Chapel in Douglasville, PA, served at the mission church in Jersey City, started the church in Belvidere and had successfully moved First Baptist Church from its original location to the new building in Lopatcong Township. After giving him all this information and answering some of his questions relative to my previous experiences at Douglasville and Jersey City, starting the church in Belvidere and all that was involved in the growth of the church in Phillipsburg, he informed me that he was on the Board of Trustees at Crossroads Bible College and Graduate School of Divinity. He was going to submit my name as a recipient for an honorary Doctor of Divinity Degree based on my Christian Service. This took place on May 30th, 1978.

In the summer of 1979 Elaine and I planned a trip with Roxann and Rick to Disney World in Florida. My father-in-law's sister and her husband had moved to Florida several years before to live with their daughter and her husband. Marilyn and Gene High had remodeled their garage into a cozy apartment for her parents. My father-in-law, Earl had not seen his sister or her family for many years. Elaine and I decided that we would ask them to join us on this trip to Florida. They were eager to go but had to wait until his vacation week near the end of August. We knew we would be driving at the hottest time of the year and our car did not have air-conditioning. We came up with a plan that would enable us to have sufficient room for all of us and afford us comfort with air-conditioning. We rented a Ford station wagon equipped with air-conditioning and a roof rack. Our entire luggage was covered with a heavy plastic covering and secured to the roof racks. This gave the entire back of the station wagon as a play and sleep area for Roxann and Rick.

We made it to Boca Raton, Florida in two days. It was extremely hot during the trip and the car air-conditioner was not working entirely to what I thought was its potential. On the second day of our vacation we all went to a park near a body of water. Eugene, Marilyn and their children were with us for the outing. For some reason or other my mother-in-law was the only one bothered by the fire ants. She was badly bitten on the arms and legs. Apart from her discomfort the outing was enjoyable.

Another highlight of our Florida trip was a boat ride up the waterway from Boca Raton. Eugene and his family, Clarence and Bertha, Donald and Gladys and their boys plus all of our family boarded the boat about 4:00 pm. It was a beautiful ride watching all the large homes and their boats tied at their docks. On the trip up the waterway the Master of Ceremonies led us in some songs. He asked if anyone aboard had an anniversary. I shouted out: "My mother-in-law." They all joined in and sang "Happy Anniversary" to her. Next he asked if anyone on board was celebrating a birthday. Again I shouted, "My mother-in-law." They all joyfully sang "Happy Birthday" to her. The only problem was that my mother-in-law was neither celebrating an anniversary nor her birthday. (Of course the rest of the passengers didn't know that.)

We prepared to leave Boca Raton and drive to Disney World in Orlando. The entire luggage was neatly loaded and covered with plastic for the short trip. Roxann and Rick had the entire back of the station wagon for themselves. We enjoyed the time we spent at Disney but noticed that Rick wasn't feeling well. The next day we left Disney and Rick still was not any better. We decided to stop at Bob and Evelyn Brooks' home in Landrum, SC. Rick's asthma problem was giving him some trouble and we didn't have any medicine that he needed with us. We called our pediatrician back home and he called in a prescription immediately.

After taking the medicine Rick began to feel much better. To prepare to spend the night with the Brooks our luggage had to be unloaded from the roof of the station wagon. When my in-laws saw their suitcase they pointed out that there was a burnt hole on the top of the suitcase. My mother-in-law opened the suitcase and saw a small burnt hole through her dress. The dress was hung on a metal clothes hanger which was packed just under the cover of the suitcase. I said that we had experienced hot weather driving to Florida but it seemed hotter driving from Florida back to South Carolina. The sun rays had beaten on the fabric of the suitcase with enough heat to cause the metal clothes hanger to become hot enough to burn a hole through the fabric of the suitcase and also the material of her dress.

Early the next morning we said our goodbyes to the Brook's and began our trip back home. The rest of the trip went well. We returned the rental station wagon and said we would long remember our Florida trip with all of the excitement and adventure.

It was during my years of tenure as Pastor of First Baptist Church in Phillipsburg, NJ that I served on the boards of: Military Evangelism,

Eastern Independent Church Mission and Fellowship of Independent Missions. It was also during my tenure that we were contacted by four pulpit committees to consider becoming their pastor. I had never put out a resume indicating that I would consider making a change and move from First Baptist Church. One pulpit committee from Indiana called me to see if I would be preaching on a certain Sunday. They wanted to make the trip to hear me preach. The day came and two members of the committee were there for the service. After the service they took Elaine and me to dinner. They had prepared a packet of information that they wanted us to read over telling of the history of the church and city. They asked us to pray about the possibility of considering becoming a candidate as pastor for their church. We said we would consider it and pray for the Lord's guidance. This meeting with the men became a real challenge as Elaine and I spoke about it together. I often had made the remark from the pulpit that I believed God had sent me to First Baptist and I was committed to be their pastor until I died, until the rapture or until he had somewhere else for me to serve. It had to be very clear to me because I was a stubborn Dutchman. Some weeks passed and I didn't feel that I wanted to explore the possibility of making a change at this time. However the pulpit committee was persistent with phone calls and letters wanting me to come and speak as a candidate. I finally agreed to come only as a pulpit supply and to speak for a Wednesday night prayer service.

I did follow through with that commitment. I spoke on a Wednesday night and after the service I met briefly with the pulpit committee and members of the elder board. It served as an introductory meeting in preparation for the official meeting to be held the following evening.

Thursday morning two elders met me for breakfast and filled me in on the history of the church, etc. They spent the day taking me through the church facilities and driving around the city showing me points of interest.

The interview meeting went well and I seemed to answer their questions satisfactorily. They in turn answered mine as well. After the meeting, several of the men took me to see the Sears Tower in

Chicago. It was quite a full evening. Early the next morning the same two men who picked me up at the Chicago airport took me back to the same airport. I flew back to Allentown and arrived at my home exhausted. I was eager to share the events of my trip with Elaine.

A short time after returning from the interview, I received a phone call from the chairman of the committee telling me that the committee unanimously voted for me to return and preach as a candidate. This now became a difficult time for me and for Elaine. We had served First Baptist Church for many years. We both had immersed ourselves in the programs and outreach of the church. We both spent much time soul searching and praying for the Lord's direction in this matter. I guess I was guilty of procrastinating because I was slow in giving the committee an answer. Again the chairman called and wanted us to at least consider coming there to preach. I consented under the condition that I was not coming as a candidate but simply as a guest speaker for that Sunday. This was easily arranged. Our whole family loaded up the car and drove to Hammond, Indiana. I fulfilled my promise to speak, but before we left to drive back home, the chairman and several of the committee members asked to speak with me. They requested that I agree to comeback at their expense and stay with them for a week and the following Sunday speak as a candidate. I told them I would continue to consider it and pray for the Lord's direction. You can imagine the discussions we had on the ride home.

I knew the time had come to notify the pulpit committee. I was sure that I did not feel that God was directing us to pursue their invitation to come as a candidate. I made the phone call and felt relieved that the decision had been made. The chairman thanked me and said they were disappointed at our decision but they fully understood.

It was back to our responsibilities at First Baptist Church. During our many years of ministry at that church, there were days of disappointment and discouragement but also more days of blessings and encouragement. I seriously thought I would continue to pastor at First Baptist until I reached the age of retirement, then request to remain as Pastor of Visitation. My thoughts were interrupted when I

135

received another invitation from the pulpit committee of a church in Elkhart, Indiana. Once again we wondered why I would receive a call since I never submitted a resume to any pulpit committee.

I agreed to follow the same procedure I did for Christian Fellowship Church in Hammond. I agreed to come as a guest speaker and meet with the pulpit committee.

They were very warm and cordial. The question and answer time went well. I learned a lot about their church and their goals for ministry. I used the drive back home to pray and consider if the Lord was indeed calling us to make a change in ministry. Again it was quite evident that it was not the time for to make the change. I was to continue at First Baptist Church.

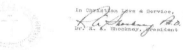

CROSSROADS GRADUATE SCHOOL
OF DIVINITY

BOB N. MAIN STREET
FARMLAND, INDIANA 47340

Dear Friend in Christ:

Upon the recommendation of the Committee of Religious Education and Bible, and by the authority vested in the Board of Directors, the CROSSROADS GRADUATE SCHOOL OF DIVINITY considers it a great pleasure to confer upon you and to present to you this Sacred Certificate bearing the title of

DOCTOR OF DIVINITY

The colors of the College are Purple and Gold. Purple — the blending of blue, that stands for truth, and red — this is symbolic of the shed blood of our Redeemer thus making the purple symbolic of ROYALTY. Gold — the basis upon which values are established, a standard upon which fineness and quality is fixed, and an element that resists tarnishings and rusts and a symbol of PURITY.

May this degree given in recognition of your calling and the furthering of God's work upon earth ever be an inspiration to you as you labor in His Vineyard.

In Christian Love & Service,

Dr. R. E. Shockney, President

Doctor of Divinity, 5-30-78

Myrtle at Florida Picnic

Return trip from Florida
at Bob Brook's home

137

# Leisure Activities

My life up to this point was exciting but busy. I did however have periods of time that I would carve out for enjoying some of my hobbies. I enjoyed hunting small game and deer. Over the years, for some reason or other, rabbits and pheasants became extinct in our area so my hunting was centered on hunting for deer. I began using a longbow and later changed to a crossbow. Some years I was successful. Then there were other years when I would return home empty-handed.

Paul and Cheryl Wentz, very good friends, bought a large house trailer and about 50 acres near Wellsboro, PA. They would invite me to join them every second week in December for doe season. It was a three-day open season. Special doe licenses were required for hunting. On several occasions Rick and Tracy joined Elaine and me. We would leave on a Sunday afternoon and arrive early in the evening. I was up early and after having a hearty breakfast, Rick and I would dress warmly and prepared to be at the designated areas as the sun began to rise. On this particular day Rick shot his first deer. He was proud to pose for a picture with Paul and myself and, of course, the doe. While we hunted, Elaine and Tracy stayed in the trailer and addressed Christmas cards. I should also mention that Cheryl was quite a hunter herself and accompanied us into the woods for the hunt. Lunch time came and we all returned to the trailer for lunch and a short rest. About 2:00 pm we once again returned to designated areas and hunted until the sun began to set.

About ten years ago on my daughter and son-in-law's property in the woods in Hellertown, we built a treehouse that would be a play house for future grandchildren but for the present I used it to hunt deer. It stood about eight feet off the ground and measured six feet by eight feet and stood eight feet high with a sloping roof line. We made our entrance by climbing up a set of stairs and opening a trap door. Handles were placed inside the wall to give you some aid in getting up into the room. Once inside you closed the trap door, laid back the carpet and took your seat on a lawn chair. The seat was covered with a hot seat. If it became too cold and chilly you simply opened one of the windows for ventilation and lit the portable propane stove for some heat. Quite comfortable I would say. Rick and I both hunted here with our crossbows but many times we went home empty-handed.

In the spring, summer and early fall, I played some golf and did a little trout fishing.

I remember in the winter of 1978 when I purchased my first snowmobile. At the time we lived at Apple Blossom Rd. and George Street in Forks Township in Easton, PA. Our home was a few short blocks from the Forks Township playground. Surrounding the playground were miles and miles of fields. We rode the snowmobile to the park taking turns learning to ride it. Later we would be familiar enough with the machine that we would ride through the fields either solo or with another member of the family on the back of the seat since the machine was big enough for two people. We enjoyed this new adventure and there was ample snow in those winter seasons to enjoy it. Taking turns riding on one machine, it wasn't long before Rick suggested it would be more fun if we had a second snowmobile so two could ride together, and carry the other two as well. My cousin Irene and her husband, Lloyd, had a cabin in the Poconos and owned several snowmobiles. In talking with her I learned that they wanted to sell one of their older machines. I eagerly bought the machine. We now could enjoy riding together. It seemed that only Rick and I enjoyed the cold so that we were mainly the only ones to ride the machines. During this time, I found an old used snowmobile trailer nearby and bought it. During the spring and summer of the following year I removed the old decking, sanded and painted the frame, installed new tires and a new heavy-duty deck. We could now easily transport both machines to other places to ride the trails.

The next winter we had a milder winter with very little snow accumulation. Rick was a student at Churchman's Business College and classes were suspended for the President's Day on February 20th. We planned a snowmobiling day together for that entire day. Promised

Land Lake had some snowmobile trails and we packed our gear and drove to there. We arrived around 9:00 am, unloaded the sleds and put on our warm clothing. The gas tanks were full and we were ready and eager to get started. After speaking with some ice fishermen, they pointed out the beginning of the trail on the opposite side of the lake. We thanked them and off we went seeking a new adventure. We reached the beginning of the trail but didn't see any signs identifying that it was indeed a snowmobile trail. There were no trail maps available which added some additional excitement. This was all virgin territory to us and no other snowmobilers were in view. Since we were there to make a day of it we began our adventure. The trail was a little rough but at least we were riding on some new territory. Eventually we came to a fork in the trail but no way to indicate where the trail would go. We took a chance and chose the right fork. After traveling for a few minutes we came to a cross section of two trails. Not knowing again where we were or where the trail would lead, we did just like we did before: we picked a trail and continued on our way.

The morning was fast slipping away and we were getting hungry and both machines needed gas. Off in the distance we saw through a break in the trees a lake with some ice fishermen. They were at their shacks fishing. We approached them to get direction for food and gas. From them we learned that what we thought was the Promised Land Lake was another lake some distance from where we originally started. They were kind enough to give us clear directions to a small town about a mile away. We reached the town without any difficulty, found a gas station where we purchased gas, some sandwiches and something to drink. The owner of the gas station drew us a rough map for directions back to Promised Land Lake. We thanked him and off we went heading back to our beginning point. Several times on our trip my snowmobile would hesitate and almost come to a stall. I would lift the back end of the machine to free the drive track, open the throttle until it gained power, let off the gas and put the sled back onto the trail. It would run good again for a while but I soon would have to repeat what I had just done. This continued until we reached Promised Land Lake. Instead of loading my sled on the trailer I told Rick I wanted to take a short run on the lake and open up the throttle to see how the engine responded. I was disappointed in the little power I had and the backfiring and popping sounds of the engine. I rode it back and stopped alongside the trailer. Next, I tried to start the engine in order to load it onto the trailer but the engine would not start. Some of the men who were standing nearby saw my problem and they helped to lift the sled onto the trailer. They were a bunch of great guys. Our day of adventure was over so we headed for home and a good hot meal. My plan was to take the sled to the dealer in Phillipsburg the following day because it was still under warranty.

Around the supper table we told Elaine about our day of adventure. She had the answer to the snowmobile problem by exclaiming that maybe God didn't want you out in the woods alone that far from home. My answer was; "If God didn't want us there the machine would have stopped far out in the woods instead of stopping right alongside the trailer."

After the dealer took a look at the problem he discovered that there was a hole that had burned into the top of the piston. He made the repairs and we were good to go. Sometime later I traded both snowmobiles in for two newer used ones.

The next year once again we didn't receive a lot of snow to ride in our area but we learned of some good trails in the Scranton area. It was the old railroad bed of the O &W railroad that ran from Scranton to the New York border. The railroad was established in 1868 but was liquidated by a U.S. bankruptcy judge in 1957. The rails and the ties were removed and a walking/bike trail was created. Later the O & W snowmobile club was organized and snowmobilers were encouraged to join the club and use the trails. Membership for a year was a very minimal fee. A construction trailer was erected for the snowmobilers to change clothing and have a place to eat lunch in the warmth of the trailer. The trails were regularly groomed with a special tractor that made the trail beds smooth. These two trails ran parallel to each other and they both were about six or seven miles long. Connecting these two trails were secondary trails that ran through woods, farm fields and into a small community. There was a small gas station and an old hotel where you could get some hot food and refuel if needed. These trails were about an hour from our home so that made the travel time manageable.

About this time Stan Britton and his wife, Norma, began attending the church. Shortly after being in attendance for a time he was rushed to the hospital with a heart problem. Upon visiting him in the hospital I learned that he loved snowmobiling and owned two machines. He belonged to a small club in Belvidere, New Jersey. He confided with me that he was very disappointed that now that this occurred, it meant he probably could never go snowmobiling again on his own. I reassured him that when he recuperated we would go snowmobiling together.

The following winter after the first sizable snow fall Stan and I drove to the O & W snowmobile club trailer, dressed into our warm snowmobile clothing and started riding the trail system. We would return several times over the winter season and on several occasions we would bring two other men from the church to ride with us. I had two machines and Stan had two so adding two others made it more of a fellowship time.

The next winter once again it turned out to be a mild winter with little or no snow to ride on the O & W trails. In doing some research on areas where they had snowmobile trails we found that Old Forge, NY was the closest to us. Old Forge, NY is located about an hour and half drive from Syracuse, NY. At first Stan and I made the trip to scout out the type of trails and gain as much information about the trails as we could. We found the cost very reasonable to register our machines. There were printed maps with clearly marked trail signs, places to get gas and a hot meal. The main trail led though the small town of Old Forge where even the police department rode snowmobiles equipped with flashing lights and sirens. The town posted speed limits for snowmobilers traveling through their streets and the police would pull you over and ticket you if you were speeding.

After one or two seasons of riding the trails in Old Forge, we were notified that the annual registration fee for our snowmobiles was to increase to an unbelievable amount that neither Stan nor I thought was worth it. We needed to find another place to run our snowmobiles. Someone suggested that we should try Redfield, NY which was located just west of Old Forge. The travel time would be the same and the fee to run the trails was very minimal.

Stan and I drove to Redfield near the Salmon River reservoir where the annual snowfall is twenty-two feet. We were told to look for the Cedar Pines Restaurant and Campgrounds and speak to the owner. Cedar Pines was located on the edge of town in a very quaint old building. Around the building was a parking lot and beyond the parking lot were several small cabins, travel trailers and a band shell. Vacationers would rent the cabins and trailers for their getaway. The band shell equipped with a stage provided musical entertainment in the spring and summer seasons.

During the snowmobile season the cabins were available to rent. We found Jerry, the owner, very friendly and he answered all our questions. He told us that they are very busy with snowmobilers over the winter weekends and that he closed on Mondays to get some rest. In our discussion with him he suggested that if we wanted to come to use the trails on a Monday that we could park our trailer on his parking lot and he would even leave the back door of his restaurant open for us. That door led to a small hallway where the restroom and the telephone were located. The hallway was heated and we could use that space to change into our snowmobile suits.

While we were there he also gave us applications to register our snowmobiles and the map of all the trails. Jerry told me that I should call him on Sunday and he would tell me about the conditions of the trails or if there had been a problem that would keep us from driving the distance to Redfield. Stan and I returned home and made arrangements to leave the next Monday and try out the trails. I called Jerry on Sunday afternoon and he gave us the all clear to drive up the next day. He would have the back door open for us and told us to have a good time on the trails.

We left Stan's house at 4:00 am. We stopped for breakfast at a diner at Tannersville on Rt. 80. A few hours later we were unloading my two sleds at Cedar Pines. We found the back door unlocked as he said and quickly dressed into our snowmobile suits. We were excited to begin our adventure on new trails with about four feet of packed snow on the trail.

After riding about an hour looking at the picturesque scenery we came to a small community with several vacation cabins and a few occupied houses. One large house was called the Sportsmen's Club. In front of this house was a very large pond with thick frozen ice. Along the banks of the pond we saw many deer feeding on food that the Sportsmen's Club owner was shoveling out to them from a small tractor pulling a cart filled with some kind of feed. He finished feeding the deer and came over us to. He asked us if we were hungry and invited us into the basement of his house which served as the dining room and bar. What a surprise we had when we approached the door into the basement. We had to walk down four steps that were built out of snow. This showed us how deep the snow was on the trails. The room was warm and we enjoyed one of the best hamburgers I have ever had. After our meal and a couple of minutes of chatting with the owner we were on our way. We followed the map and took the trails that would take us in a circle bringing us back to Cedar Pines. Here we dressed into our street clothes and began our trip home. It was a long day but we had never seen so much snow and so many groomed trails to ride.

The next trip we planned we invited John Harrold and Gary Droppa to join us. Stan took his two machines and I took mine. John Harrold's wife, Dottie, made two large thermoses of soup and sent it with us with some rolls, plastic cups and spoons. Before we started on the trail I fastened the two thermoses next to the motor of my snowmobile. I had a small glove compartment in the back of my machine where we stored the rolls, the plastic cups and spoons.

After riding for some time we came to a place where our trail intersected with another. We stopped and I took out the rolls and the plastic cups and spoons. I handed the thermoses to John who filled our cups with the good hot soup. The rolls tasted good with the soup. When we had finished we washed the cups and spoons in the snow and placed them back in the compartment in the back of my sled. I don't know how many miles we rode that day, but as the day began to come to an end we managed to reach Cedar Pines in good time. Soon we were back on the highway heading for home.

On another occasion Rick and I made the trip to Cedar Pines and had another great day enjoying riding the trails on our snowmobiles.

After several trips to Cedar Pines we thought it not fair for Jerry to make sure the back door of the restaurant was opened for our use. We never bought a meal or filled our snowmobiles with the gas from his pumps because he was closed the day we were there. All agreed that we should show him our appreciation by collecting some money and presenting him with our gift. We all joyfully gave generously. Before we left to come home that day we went over to his residence and knocked on the door. When he answered the door we were all standing there as we presented the gift to him. We expressed our sincere appreciation for his kindness and generosity but we felt badly because we could not patronize him since we always came on Monday and he was closed for business. We wanted to show how much being able to use his facilities meant to us and presented him with our gift. He initially refused but we insisted and he graciously accepted.

It was only about a year later in 1990 that I resigned from the church and my snowmobiling days to my favorites spot ended. I sold my trailer and snowmobiles to Gary Droppa.

A few years after selling my snowmobiles to Gary he invited me to join him to return to Redfield. By this time Gary had bought a small cabin and erected a small garage to hold his tractor equipped with a large bucket. When he wanted to go there to go snowmobiling, he would have to park on the road in front of his cabin, wade waste deep in the snow back to the garage and use his tractor to clear a parking place and an entrance to his cabin. Now it is some 26 years later that I am writing my story and these memories are still fresh in my mind.

Rich's first deer: Paul
Wentz, Rick and me

Tree house for hunting

Rick on our first
snowmobile

O&W Trails, Scranton, PA

Me riding on O&W Trails

Cedar Pines, Redfield, NY

Snowmobile trails,
Redfield, NY

Snowmobile groomer,
Redfield, NY

148

Stan Britton & John
Harrold soup break

Gary Droppa's cabin

Snowmobiling at Gary
Droppa's cabin

# Family Activities

While I was still Pastor of First Baptist Church of Phillipsburg, NJ, two important birthdays were rapidly approaching. My dad would be celebrating his 75th birthday in 1984 and my father-in-law celebrating his 80th birthday in 1985.

Tom Linder was a member of our church who had recently moved to Maine to start a popcorn business using a kiosk in a shopping center as his starting point. He would specialize in making popcorn in a variety of flavors. In our correspondence back and forth he told me of this new adventure and wondered if I would ever visit him in the future. I explained that I wanted to treat my dad to something special for his 75th birthday. Tom suggested that I fly him on People's Express operating out of Newark airport. They had a very low-cost flight from Newark to Logan airport in Boston. He would be happy to meet us there and take us on a tour of the historical sites of Boston.

I looked into the cost of the flight and found out that it was very inexpensive. A round trip ticket was very feasible and so dad's 75th birthday present was decided. It would take us longer to drive to Newark airport than to fly from Newark to Boston. Total time of the flight was 1 hr. and 5 minutes.

The day arrived and I picked up my dad at his apartment in Emmaus very early that morning. We drove to a restaurant near the airport for breakfast before boarding the plane to Boston. As soon as we found our seats the stewardess approached us with a credit card machine. People's Express did not have ticket agents or a counter at the airport in order to keep the cost of the ticket low. I presented my credit card. The stewardess swiped my card through the machine and we were ready for takeoff.

We had an enjoyable flight. It was my dad's first plane trip and he thoroughly enjoyed it. Upon arrival at the designated gate I told my dad to remain in his seat because the passengers all wanted to be the first ones off the plane. It wasn't long when it was our time to leave our seats. As we approached the cabin exit door the pilot greeted us as he was leaving the cockpit and asked us how we enjoyed the flight. I told him that it was my father's 75th birthday and his first trip ever on an airplane. He asked us to step off the plane but remain on the jetway. In a few minutes he motioned for us to come back on the plane. He told my dad to take a seat in the copilot's seat while he sat in the pilot's seat explaining many of the flight instruments. My dad was delighted and thanked the pilot for his kindness.

As we came to the end of the jetway we saw Tom Linder patiently waiting for us. After exchanging greetings and introducing my dad we explained that we were late leaving the plane because the pilot was explaining to my dad the instruments in the cockpit from the co-pilot's seat.

Once out of the airport, Tom took us on a tour of the historical sites of Boston. He took us to one of the restaurants to taste Boston's famous baked beans. At the end of the day we celebrated dad's birthday with a seafood dinner in a restaurant on one of the docks. After a great meal Tom drove us back to the airport to catch our plane back to Newark. We boarded the plane, took our seats and paid for our ticket in the same manner as on our trip to Boston. In a short time we arrived back at Newark, found our car and I drove dad back to his apartment. What a great end to a terrific day.

The next adventure was to plan something for my father-in-law's 80th birthday to be celebrated in 1985, just a few months away. I remembered that grandpa (that's what we always called him) loved trains. So I planned to take him to New York City and take the Amtrak train to Washington, DC.

After making all the arrangements and checking into the train schedule, we left Allentown very early in the morning and started on our journey. Our first stop was the Pancake House in Phillipsburg for their delicious pancake breakfast. We knew that this big breakfast

151

would have to tie us over until we could find lunch somewhere in Washington, DC.

We parked the car at the Port of Authority Garage in Jersey City, NJ. We took the elevator down to the platform of the subway station. We rode the subway train to Pennsylvania Station at 34th and 7$^{th}$ Avenues in New York City. Grandpa always liked to ride the first car of the subway and look out the front door window as the train moved through the tunnel under the Hudson River and into Pennsylvania Station. After purchasing our roundtrip tickets we boarded the train for Washington, DC. It would take us just a few minutes under three hours to enjoy the smooth train ride and watch the scenery whiz by. We enjoyed a cup of coffee and some pastry from the dining car as we experienced the thrill of the train ride.

The train came to stop and we disembarked onto the loading platform. Outside the station we caught a jitney that we would use to take us around the city to the many historical sites. We visited the Washington Monument, the Lincoln Memorial, the Jefferson Memorial, the U.S. Capital building, the White House, the Supreme Court and the Smithsonian Museum. Most of our stops were brief in order to see as many as possible in our short stay in the city. We did however take the time to tour some of the Smithsonian Museum.

As we walked around some of the sights, I remember we both were getting hungry. I can't remember where we were or on what street, but I remember walking for quite a distance looking for anything that looked like a place to get something to eat. Since it was Grandpa's birthday celebration we were looking for a cafeteria. (Grandpa always liked eating at a cafeteria.) It seemed we walked for quite a while and to no avail. Then we approached a man in a business suit carrying an attaché case. I stopped him to ask if he knew of a place to eat in that area of the city, preferably a cafeteria. He informed us that we were, believe it not, standing between two cafeterias, one on either side of the street. To our right was the old Health and Welfare building with a cafeteria on the bottom floor. To our left was the new Health and Welfare building with a cafeteria on the top floor with a view of some

152

of the city. We elected to cross the street and enter the new Health and Welfare building. We entered the foyer of the building and were greeted by a security guard who requested that we show him our identification badges. I explained who we were and told him we were celebrating my father-in-law's 80th birthday by visiting the city. We simply wanted to get some lunch and be on our way. I told him I would be happy to show him my clergy identification if that would be sufficient for him to allow us to go to the cafeteria. He simply smiled and directed us to the elevator that would take us to the top floor and the cafeteria. We took the time to see what was available in this rather swanky looking cafeteria and both decided on a roast beef dinner. What a dinner it was. As we exited the building we thanked the security guard for his kindness. Needless to say, this made Grandpa quite happy.

The rest of the day we continued to tour the sites, riding the jitney. Our last stop was back to Union Station to board the Amtrak train back to New York City. The train ride was uneventful until we came into the Newark, NJ station. The conductor came on the loud speaker system to inform us that we would have to leave the train and take the subway into Pennsylvania Station in New York City because the overhead power line was down between Newark and New York City.

The wait for the subway wasn't too long and we were boarding the subway train to Pennsylvania Station in New York City. Fortunately for us the first stop on the subway ride would be at Jersey City before continuing to New York City, so we could get off at Jersey City and not have to go into Pennsylvania station in order to take the PATH Train back to Jersey City.

After arriving at the Journal Square Station in Jersey City, we took the elevator up to the floor of the garage and found our car. In another hour and a half, we were safely back in Allentown, after a long and exhausting but great day of celebration.

It wasn't long after the two trips to celebrate two birthdays that Ed Savacool Sr. informed me that his son, Lieutenant Colonel Edwin

Savacool Jr., had requested that Ed and I come to visit him at the Pentagon. He wanted to take us on a tour of the facilities.

When all the arrangements were finalized, we drove to the parking lot of the Pentagon. It is amazing how large a facility we were looking at. Ed said he knew which door we were to enter and so we began walking in that direction. Upon finding the door it was amazing to see a beautiful door blocked with magnificent stonework. I guess we got to the wrong door. We started back the way we came and followed another sidewalk toward another entrance door. As we approached, the door opened and a uniformed serviceman held the door open for us. We thanked him and walked inside. We were in the gymnasium. Ed immediately went to the desk and asked to use the telephone. He called Ed Jr.'s office and were told to stay where we were and he would come to get us. Later as we were leaving the gym Ed Jr. told us that we were in a restricted area.

Ed Jr. took us on a short tour and then to lunch. We had the privilege to eat lunch with the Generals and high-ranking officers. This was a real treat to say the least. Ed Jr.'s rank was Lieutenant Colonel.

Ed Jr. had to return to his office to attend to matters so he set us up with a young ensign who was about to start a tour with another group. It was interesting to listen to the tour guide explain the function and statistics of the Pentagon. The Pentagon has 17.5 miles of corridors with the total floor area of 6.6 million sq. ft. The building is five stories above ground and two stories underground. To aid in moving from one corridor to another there is a fleet of self-propelled scooters that average 3 mph. The Pentagon is a five-sided building of individual corridors with a court yard called "Ground Zero" in the center.

While walking in one of the inner corridors we could look down to see military personnel in the courtyard. Our tour guide stopped for us to look down more closely to the courtyard area. He explained that they had a serious problem with the pigeons flying around in the courtyard and there were problems with all the pigeon dirt left on benches and the pavements. They tried to smoke them out, but that didn't work. Next, they tried playing loud music but that also was a waste of time. So they decided to run an ad in the newspaper offering a $3,000.00 reward to anyone who could successfully remove the pigeons from the courtyard area.

A few weeks later an Amish man from Lancaster came with a large cardboard box. He asked for a step ladder and climbed to the top of the gazebo in the center of the courtyard. He opened the box and removed a large plastic owl. After securing the owl to the roof of the gazebo he climbed back down the ladder and was escorted into the building to collect the reward. It was estimated that the owl cost the Amish man less than $20.00.

When the tour was concluded, we went back to say goodbye to Lieutenant Colonel Edwin Savacool Jr. and made our way back home.

Over the years at First Baptist Church it became evident that I could no longer be involved in all the ministries and activities of the growing congregation. It was time to add additional staff. We already had hired a full-time secretary and now it was time to call an assistant pastor to share in the needs of the ministry.

The first assistant pastor was a recent graduate from Philadelphia College of Bible. He and his wife would be primarily working with the young people and guide them in the church activities. They were the first of several to serve over the next several years.

Working alongside these men greatly assisted me as well as giving them the satisfaction of a ministry. But all of that changed about 1988. At that time there were two assistant pastors serving the church programs. One served in the ministry of Music and Christian Education and the other served in youth ministries. It became evident that things were not going as smoothly as in previous years. There seemed to be tension in the air.

Every Monday morning I would hold a staff meeting with the other two pastors. Each had their individual responsibilities and ministries. It was at these meeting we would review their goals and vision for the ministries. I would discuss with them pertinent information and things on my mind and agenda. We would also talk together of problems or concerns that anyone of us had on our minds and hearts.

The tension continued to build and at the next elder board meeting I informed the elders that since there is a desire to take a different approach to the vison and ministry of the church I could no longer consider remaining as the senior pastor. The board insisted that the church needed all three of us to continue in our various ministries. However I will not elaborate on the events of the previous months only to say that as the Pastor the spirit of the church greatly concerned me.

My dad and me in Boston for his 75th birthday

# Leaving the Pastorate

While I pastored at First Baptist I also served on the several boards mentioned previously. It was at one of the Board of Director's meetings of Fellowship of Independent Missions that the change in my life and ministry came to be. For some time at those board meetings we had discussed the possibility of seeking someone to join the director to assist him in his responsibilities. Paul Platt was the Director of FIM and had served in the capacity for many years. Paul was in his 80's and because of his age and the health condition of his wife he was neither able to attend missions' conferences on behalf of FIM nor recruit new candidates in Bible Colleges and seminaries. He was only able to run the daily duties of the office (which he did quite thoroughly).

At most of the board meetings it seemed that we only had a few minutes to discuss what action we should take to meet the need before we needed to go on to other pressing business matters. I made it my responsibility to attend every board meeting if at all possible. However, it was at one of those board meetings I was not able to attend that the board had more time to discuss the help needed and the future of the mission. That night after the board meeting had ended I received several phone calls from the president and other members telling me that they had discussed at length the possibility of me coming to serve as Assistant Director. They wanted me to meet with the executive committee to discuss the position of Assistant Director. Was this God's way of moving me to another ministry? Was it time for me to leave a ministry to which I had dedicated my life? Had I served the Lord with all my heart and life as a pastor and now would I embark on a new ministry in missions? Missions had always been my heartbeat ever since I became a pastor. I would need to share this with Elaine and together seek the mind of the Lord for our future.

After much prayer and our talks together both Elaine and I knew that this invitation to become a part of FIM was God's will for our lives. I called the President of the Board of FIM, Bill Simpkins, and a meeting was setup with the executive committee.

I met with the executive committee and a job description of sorts was agreed upon. The question of salary was discussed and after a brief time a figure was agreed upon which was less than we had received as Pastor of First Baptist Church. The problem was that the mission had a limited amount of funds to be applied to my salary. The rest would have to be raised by me. I felt comfortable with the arrangements because all of our mission family members had to raise their support as well. The board agreed to make up the difference of my salary that I could not raise. I was able to raise about 60% of my salary from family, friends and several churches. Elaine contributed greatly to our salary needs with her position as surgical assistant to an oral surgeon.

I submitted my resignation to the church family to become effective June 1st, 1990. The last Sunday that I preached the church was filled and it was difficult for me to conduct the final service of my 24 years of ministry at First Baptist Church. It took a long time for the people to leave the church after the conclusion of the service saying goodbye at the door. Finally all the people were gone and I prepared to leave the church for the last time. I left with some sadness but no bitter feelings toward anyone because I knew in my heart that God was definitely leading me into another ministry.

In hindsight I shall always remember the spirit of love and cooperation that I experienced from the people in the twenty-four years that I served as Pastor beginning with that small flock and continually building to the size it was when I resigned. There were many highlights to remember but I will only mention a few:

1. In 1971 – A banquet was held at Walp's Restaurant celebrating my 5th year of ministry at First Baptist. Elaine and I were surprised when Ed Dickey called us up front in the banquet room and told us the church was sending us to Word of Life in Schroon Lake, NY in appreciation of our ministry.

2. In 1976 – A surprise service to celebrate our 10$^{th}$ anniversary at First Baptist Church.

3. In 1980 – The celebration of our 25$^{th}$ wedding anniversary.

4. In 1982 – The celebration of 25 years in the ministry.

5. Our 25$^{th}$ Wedding anniversary trip to Bermuda with a group from the church. About 22 people flew with us from Newark. We stayed at the Hamilton Hotel on Main Street. The weather was great. We all had lots of fun.

6. The celebration of "This Is Your Life." A lot of effort went into this surprise. Many old friends were in attendance. A tape recording was played from my former Pastor, Rev. C. Leslie Miller, and another recording from my Bob Jones roommate, Dick Williams.

7. We took two other trips to Bermuda with a group from the church. One was a cruise; another was to Willow Bank, located at the far end of the island. We all rented motor scooters and toured the island. After our evening meal, Jim Alexander, Ed Savacool, Paul Heller and I took a ride to show Paul Heller the lighthouse at the other end of the island. This was Paul's first trip to Bermuda and we all had been there once before. We told our wives we should be back by 10:00 pm. It was quite a ride, a little farther than we had planned. Remember Bermuda pulls in the sidewalks around 5:00 pm. All gas stations and small places of business are closed for the day. The evening meal is always served around 7:00 pm. We left after the evening meal reaching the lighthouse at 10:30 pm. The problem we faced now was that it would take another hour and a half to two hours to ride back to the hotel. We didn't have cell phones and no place was open that might have a phone. On top of that the hotel would not receive calls after 8:00 pm.

159

So we were in hot water and decided the best thing to do would be ride back and face the music.

Now the fun started. After riding for about a half an hour we lost Paul. We stopped and turned around only to find him on the side of the road out of gas. No gas stations were open so we locked the scooter to a pole and Paul rode along with Jim. We were almost home when we lost Ed. So we stopped again and turned around only to find Ed on the side of the road with a flat tire. There was only one thing to do. Lock the scooter to a pole so Ed rode back with me. By the time we all got back to the Hotel it was almost midnight. I went to our room and all the wives were sitting there with Elaine. As I walked into the room and seeing all the wives glaring at me I wasn't expecting the greeting I receive from Elaine. With her eyes as big as saucers she looked me in the eye and said: "Well, let's hear your excuse." I thought about what took place and started to bust out laughing. In between breaths, because I was laughing so hard, I muttered, "We ran out of gas and had a flat tire." I know that was an old excuse used many times by others but it was the truth. The room got deadly silent and the other wives went to their rooms to face their own husbands.

The new ministry to which the Lord led me was to serve as Associate Director of Fellowship of Independent Missions. FIM's office was located in an office complex just off Route One in Langhorne, PA. Paul Platt was easy to work with and the girls in the office received me gladly. The office staff consisted of Paul Platt, the Director, one full-time secretary and three part-time helpers. Paul wanted me to work with him two days a week in Langhorne and I could work from my home on the other days. The office hours at Langhorne were set at 9:00 am to 3:00 pm. I spent the time learning the office procedure and assisting Paul in any way he chose. Sometimes I answered calls from missionaries or churches needing to have some information. I began compiling a mailing list for the purpose of sending out a prayer letter seeking financial support.

Several months before I was called to appear before the executive committee we had a decision to make as a full board. Paul Platt had received from a lady at the church he was attending the opportunity to receive her car as a gift to the mission. She had been in a slight accident and knew it was time to give up the car. We had a lengthy discussion about the pros and cons of receiving the car. It appeared that we all agreed that there really wasn't a need to have a car that no one would drive and have all the expense of title transfer and insurance. Amazingly enough when the vote was taken it was unanimous to receive the car. Now that I was part of the leadership of FIM the car was given to me to drive on mission business.

I began visiting some pastors that supported FIM missionaries. Many of these visits were times of answering questions relative to the activities of the missionary. It was difficult to have the missionary family respond regularly to the board's requirement of monthly reports. It turned out that these visits formed a bonding relationship between the supporting church, the missionary and FIM, the sending agent. I began receiving invitations to attend the church missionary conferences, speaking at Bible Institutes and colleges and as a pulpit supply.

As I became more and more familiar with the office procedure, I was aware of some changes that would make the business end more proficient. The entire bookkeeping system was done without computers. This required several of the part-time girl's hours of manually writing out receipts, etc.

After I had served with Paul Platt for about a year, he submitted his resignation as General Director of FIM. He had served faithfully for many years and was now looking forward to retirement. I was given the position of leadership under the title of General Director.

One of the first matters of business was to upgrade the ancient bookkeeping system to computer management. I learned of a retired missionary from North Carolina who had moved his missions' agency from the manual bookkeeping system to computers. He agreed to come to the Langhorne office and transfer all of our records onto the computer.

It was at this same time that Ray Shive who had served as a missionary in South Africa joined the FIM missionary family. He was not interested in returning to South Africa but was willing to assist in the home office. The board interviewed Ray and his wife Ruth and accepted them to serve with me in the home office. Ray was computer savvy and agreed to work with the gentleman from North Carolina in setting up the new record system on computers.

New Year's Day Elaine and I visited with her parents in Allentown. Her mother was very friendly with one of the ladies from Bethel Bible Fellowship Church. She and her husband owned several acres of land near Coplay. They learned that I had been looking for a place that the mission could own rather than rent. The facilities at Langhorne that the mission rented were quite expensive and did not have any place for visiting missionaries or candidates to stay. My plan was to have a place that would double for office facilities and a hospitality unit for visiting missionaries or candidates. This couple invited me to drive with them to see the area that they owned. They were willing to give us as much land as we needed to build an office complex and hospitality unit. I then contacted an engineer friend of mine to give me the cost for surveying and subdividing the area.

A few days later I had an opportunity to be in Allentown and driving down 24th Street, I saw a large home that was for sale. I saw many homes in my life that were up for sale so I drove by but couldn't get it out of my mind. After driving past the house for about a mile, I felt that I had to turn around and inquire about the house.

I was able to walk though and see the potential for what we needed for offices and a hospitality unit. The owner had the house built to meet his needs as a builder. You couldn't see it from the outside but the first floor had his office, a secretary's office, a small family room with fireplace, a kitchen, a dining room and another large sitting room with

162

a fireplace and a powder room. The second floor had a very large master bedroom suite, a large bedroom that his four boys had shared when they were home, two smaller bedrooms, a full bath and a small sewing room. The large third floor attic was unfinished.

When I returned to my office in Langhorne I received the quote from the engineer who surveyed the property in Coplay. The price to do what needed to be done for us to begin to build a building was $30,000.00 and we hadn't even turned a spade of dirt. The house on 24th Street was listed at $350,000.00, and we could move right in and use it just as it was.

I called the executive committee together for a meeting to visit the land and walk through the house. We met at Cedar Crest Bible Fellowship Church for a time of prayer and introduction to what led to the offer of the land and my tour of the house on 24th street.

After we all saw the land and walked through the house it was the unanimous decision of the executive committee to call the full board together to finalize the next move.

The full board heard the report from the executive committee and unanimously agreed to pursue making an offer for the purchase of the house. Jack Sullivan, the mission treasurer, and I were appointed to follow up with the real estate agent for purchasing the house.

Jack and I found out from the real estate agent that doctors and lawyers that lived in the vicinity of the house wanted to purchase it for their practices. However the city fathers turned them down because there was insufficient parking area.

An offer was made to the real estate agent far below the asking price and we waited to hear the response of the owner. Amazingly enough he accepted our offer because the house had been on the market for a considerable amount of time with no other offers but ours. Now we needed to arrange for a mortgage.

I made an appointment to meet with the president of the bank that we as a church had used in Phillipsburg, NJ. I explained what we wanted to do with the property and the amount we requested for a mortgage. I also stressed that we would appreciate him considering a low percentage rate.

In a short time after I met with the bank president, he agreed to the amount requested for our mortgage at a very low rate. Naturally the board of directors accepted the offer and we were now ready to proceed. However we were not able to move ahead because the neighbors had hired a lawyer and were opposing us purchasing the property. So the city fathers informed us that we needed to appear before them in a public meeting to review our request to purchase the property.

This meant that we needed to hire a lawyer to be present with us for the meeting. The meeting was set. Jack Sullivan, our lawyer and I attended the public meeting. Other business was discussed and then finally the chairman of the committee called me to come to the front to answer questions.

After all the questions were answered I was dismissed and the meeting ended. The next morning I received a call from our lawyer that the lawyer from the neighbors who opposed us had informed him that all opposition was dropped. We were cleared to proceed with finalizing the purchase.

While the paper work was drawn up and prior to the settlement date, I now needed to think about moving the office from Langhorne up to our new home in Allentown. In speaking with the existing secretaries in Langhorne, they were unable to move with the office to Allentown. This would be a problem to find qualified people to work with us in Allentown. But it is amazing how God can work out even the smallest detail. I was able to hire Nancy Krauss as full-time secretary, Barbara Boyer and Diane Snyder as part-time secretaries.

Schroon Lake at
Word of Life

10th Anniversary in New
Building with Andy Telford

25th Wedding Anniversary

This is Your Life
Celebration

Paul Pratt

Me as Associate Director

FIM Headquarters,
Allentown PA

New FIM General Director

# Visiting Family

When Alexis was 8 years old, M&M Mars transferred Rick to the Ethel M plant in Henderson, NV. Rick had been at the main office of M&M in Hackettstown, NJ for about ten years when the move was made. Rick and Tracy found a nice house on a quiet street in Henderson and set up housekeeping. Alexis walked to school a few blocks from their home. The center of Las Vegas was a short distance from their new home along with a few shopping centers and many fine restaurants. They had settled in a good location.

Elaine and I now needed to work out a plan to visit with them. We no longer could get in the car and drive a mile or two to their home in Easton. It wasn't long after they had moved to Henderson that Elaine and I flew out for a brief visit. We really enjoyed the weather and the location of their new home. We visited the church that they had been attending and enjoyed the service. The Pastor and people were very warm and friendly.

The following year we decided to drive out. Of course this suited me to no end because I really enjoy driving. Believe it or not, I can relax no matter the condition of the road or the traffic problems. This time we planned our trip over the Easter season because Alexis would be home from school on their spring break. Enroute we planned a stopover at Zanesville, OH and a brief stay with our old friends Buzz and Beverly Benson. While with the Bensons we toured the Longaberger Basket factory in Newark, OH.

After leaving the Benson's home we had made arrangements to meet with my roommate from Bob Jones, Dick Williams. He now was a Professor in the Reading Department at the University of Oklahoma. We met for lunch at a Cracker Barrel near his home. It was great to see him again and reminisce about our college days and the summer I spent with him in Phoenix, AZ.

After saying our goodbyes we started out again for our destination to Henderson, NV. We were happy to arrive at their home and looking forward to our visit. This visit would be longer than the other two.

Rick arranged for us to take a tour of the facilities at the Ethel M Plant. Some years earlier, Mr. Mars had built this state-of-the-art chocolate factory to produce a very high grade of chocolate candies. He named the plant after his mother, Ethel. These candies are not available in stores and can only be purchased through their catalogue sales department. The plant is surrounded on the outside with a variety of beautiful cactus plants.

One morning while reading the local newspaper, I saw an ad for a train ride to the Grand Canyon. The train would leave the station at Williams, AZ and travel to the Grand Canyon. Williams, AZ was a three-hour car ride from their home in Henderson. After talking it over we all agreed to make the trip. I purchased the tickets and made reservation at a motel in Williams for a two-night stay. The trip went without any problems. After checking into the motel we found a restaurant and enjoyed our evening meal.

The next morning after breakfast we walked to the Grand Canyon Railroad station to board the train. The train would leave at 9:30 am and arrive at the south end of the canyon at 11:45 am. During the train ride we were entertained by a cowboy singing western songs accompanied by him playing the guitar. About half way to our destination the train was stopped by a band of masked bandits. We could see them riding alongside the train on their horses before the train came to a stop. Of course all of this was preplanned. The bandits came through all the cars waving their unloaded guns and asking for money like they used to do in the frontier days.

It was a warm and sunny day even though we only had a short time to sightsee the wonders of the canyon. But all this was worth the trip. At 3:30 pm we were once again boarding the Grand Canyon Train enroute back to Williams, AZ. We would arrive back at the Williams station at 5:45 pm. After another delicious meal we retired to our motel rooms and prepared for the return trip to Henderson early the next morning.

On our return trip we drove to see the magnificent sights of the Hoover Dam. This was a wonderful climax to a great trip we enjoyed as a family.

A few days after our trip to the Grand Canyon and before Alexis returned to school, the three of us took a short trip to the snow-covered Mt. Charleston. We had to dress warmly because the temperature was a lot colder than when we left Henderson. It was great fun making snowballs and running in the snow.

Soon it was time for us to say our goodbyes and begin our return trip back to Macungie. Driving back through Williams we encountered a whiteout. It was hard to believe that a few days earlier we were there enjoying the sun on a warm day. Although the trip was a lot longer driving than when we flew, we enjoyed the scenery and after that brief snow squall the weather was bright and sunny the rest of the way home.

About a year after this visit, Rick was transferred back to Hackettstown, NJ. It wasn't long after receiving his transfer that they found a wonderful home in Forks Township in Easton, PA, where they continue to live to this day.

Rick and Tracy's home in Henderson, NV

Grand Canyon Train

Me at the Grand Canyon

# Moving the FIM Office

Ray Shive had been invited to speak at a church in Philadelphia and during his message he mentioned moving to Allentown and seeking qualified office personnel. At the conclusion of the service Ray was approached by a young woman who had a friend serving as the business manager of a Christian school. The school had notified him that they were closing and he needed to find another position. At the same time I had contacted Cedar Crest Bible Fellowship Church and Nancy Taylor who attended Faith Evangelical Free Church for a possible person who could serve as a secretary. Nancy posted the announcement on the church bulletin board and I was contacted by Nancy Krause.

Ray informed me of the contact he had made when he spoke at the church in Philadelphia. We invited the business manager to come to our Langhorne office for an interview. He explained his background and previous business experience. We explained that we would have to consider some salary but needed to receive that information from the full board. He informed us that he was receiving several months' pay from the previous school and that he was willing to come and serve without a salary for a period of time. I extended the invitation for him to live at the new location temporarily while we moved our office equipment from Langhorne and set up the office.

Next came the moving of the office equipment to our new location. Should we rent a truck and move the equipment ourselves or should we contact a moving company for an estimate on the costs for the move? I had used moving equipment from Frick Transfer on several occasions in the past. They put me on their employee list for insurance purposes even though I never received any pay from them. They would give me the use of a truck and all the equipment for replacing the fuel used. I approached Paul Robison general manager of Frick Transfer with the request for the use of a truck. To my utter amazement he offered to have his men move all of our equipment at no charge.

The day came and the move was made without a hitch. The business manager moved in and set up his office. The secretary began her duties with the new computer program. The equipment that we had in Langhorne was old and insufficient for our needs in Allentown. Elaine was working as an assistant to an oral surgeon in Easton. The real estate agent next to the surgeon's office was closing and he was retiring. He had a phone system for sale, two office desks and some other furniture. Elaine introduced me to him and we talked about his asking price for all of the office equipment. I counter offered with a lower price and a suggested plan to pay for it. I offered some cash down and set the period of time that the balance would be paid. Failure to meet the deadline for final payment would result in a 10% of the total price as a penalty. He said I was a hard man to deal with but would agree to the arrangement.

Once again Paul Robison arranged for the new office equipment to be moved to our new location.

The new office layout was as follows: The first-floor front office was for the secretaries. Next to her was the business manager's office. The office chairs and sofas that we purchased from the real estate agent were placed in the large family room with the fireplace. The upstairs corner bedroom became my office. Next to me was Ray's office. We both received new desks previously purchased from the real estate office. The large bedroom that the previous owner's four sons shared became the Board of Director's board room.

I met with other mission directors to introduce myself to our mission and learned their procedures. Several men with a mission's background became my mentors. It was a large leap for me to go from a Pastor to a mission executive. It was time to present to the Board of Directors my plan to establish a procedures and policy handbook, establish a curriculum and procedure for beginning a candidate school for new candidates. These things were not in the process of the old office procedures. We needed to move from a mission office to a bona fide mission agency.

All the information I had gathered from other agencies and my mission's friends I gave over to Ray to begin the process of compiling a mission handbook and procedures manual. He would produce a section and present it to me. We would review it together and accept it or make necessary changes. After the book was completed it was presented to the board members to read over and mark any section(s) needing to be simplified or explained. One by one the sections were reviewed by the Board, any changes made and approved. Finally the work was completed.

The next project to be tackled was the curriculum and setting up of a candidate school. During the office setup time we had received several applicants to be interviewed. Along with the new handbook and procedures manual, we updated the application forms. Each candidate was given the new application forms and procedures. When completed, I reviewed each one and if meeting our requirements I would invite them to attend a board meeting to be interviewed by the full board.

After the interview the candidate(s) were dismissed to another room to await the final word from the President of the Board. A unanimous vote was needed to extend a welcome to the FIM family. They would then be called back into the room and officially welcomed into the FIM family. The next step for them would be to attend the next candidate school.

Our first candidate school was several months after moving to our new location. It was June 1992. The candidate school was held at our facilities. Homes were opened up for the candidates to stay overnight. Their host and hostess would house them overnight and provide a breakfast for them. The rest of the meals were provided at our facility. Ruth Shive and Nancy Krauss arranged for the preparation of the meals. Friday of the week of candidate school was also a full board meeting, at which time the candidates were again interviewed by the board. After the first candidate school, we made a change in procedures. When a candidate completed their application forms and were approved by me, they were invited to the next candidate school. At the end of candidate school they would appear before the board for the first time to be interviewed.

After a candidate was approved by the board they began to seek individuals and churches to be their financial and prayer supporters. It was during the candidate school program that each missionary candidate, along with our supervision, would establish a support figure. Under the old system, whatever funds they could receive would be the amount they would be released to go to their field of ministry. As I visited those older missionaries I found that most of them were under-supported and some had taken part-time work to make ends meet. This procedure was against the agreement that a missionary had with the laws of the country where they worked. They did not have any health insurance, retirement funds or funds to return to the States on furlough.

Under our new procedures their support amount included sufficient funds for living and housing expenses, reserve furlough funds, health insurance and retirement funds. A missionary preparing to leave for their ministry destination needed to have at least 95% of the funds required. Furlough funds were held in their account in the home office. Their retirement and health insurance funds were administered by the office staff.

Since our move to Allentown from Langhorne we lost a few board members who were not able to commit to continue to faithfully serve. I began to recruit additional members. Our previous board consisted mainly of all pastors except one businessman. My goal was to recruit a few more businessmen who had a heart for missions and were able to commit themselves to serve along with one or two men who had served as missionaries. Eventually we were able to have a Board of Directors consisting of two financial men, two who served as foreign missionaries, a doctor, a lawyer and several pastors. It was a good board with many years of experience and much knowledge.

174

Things were moving along nicely. Every day was a new challenge for me. I could hardly wait to get into the office and get to work. A new challenge was now on the table. FIM had an office in Three Hills, Alberta, Canada. Their annual board meeting was always held in April. Under the old procedure all the business between the Langhorne office and Canadian office was conducted via telephone because Paul Platt was unable to personally attend due to his wife's health condition.

I made arrangements to fly from ABE to Calgary with a stopover in Chicago. When I landed at Calgary I made my way to Hertz rental booth to pick up my rental car. I had asked for the cheapest car they had listed. It was a Chevy Geo. It was small but I accepted it and was going to use it for the couple of days I would be in Canada. I would meet with the office staff to not only introduce myself but also to explain to them the procedures that were to be used in the Canadian office. I had a speaking engagement for the following Sunday in a small prairie town of Murrin.

The office staff consisted of: Margret Ewing, office manager, a part-time secretary and Steve Erickson as president. Steve had been a missionary for many years in India. He was a tall Swede with a great personality and quick sense of humor. After the staff meeting Steve took me to a small prairie town a few miles from Three Hills. It was a small community of Linden with about 500 people, all Mennonites.

Steve took me to the only restaurant in town for lunch. The restaurant was called "Country Cousins." They had a limited menu and a very small buffet table. I had something from the buffet which was tasty but the best was the dessert. They were noted for their peanut butter pie. Steve said this was the reason he brought me to this restaurant because the peanut butter pie was his favorite. After eating my piece of peanut butter pie and a cup of coffee it became my favorite dessert as well.

The next day Steve and I went to conduct some mission business that he had postponed until I arrived. Enroute Steve said that I needed to try Tim Horton coffee. I had never heard of Tim Horton and he explained that Tim was a popular Canadian hockey player that started this franchise. To my surprise I really enjoyed my first cup of Tim Horton coffee. This would be the first of several cups of Tim Horton coffee while in Canada. When I returned home I found that I could purchase Tim Horton coffee at Wegman's. Good news, now I can also get a cup at Tim Horton located in the new PPL center in downtown Allentown.

Over the next ten years I would make this trip every year to attend the Canadian annual Board of Director's meeting. Every time after picking up my rental car at the airport I would begin my trip of two hours to Three Hills. Would you believe it, I would have to pass by the cutoff to Linden on my way to Three Hills. I began to realize that every time I approached that cutoff to Linden, the car automatically turned into Linden and stopped at the Country Cousins restaurant for a cup of coffee and a piece of peanut butter pie. I learned after my first trip there that I should save some of the Canadian money that I had left over from my previous visit so that I would have at least enough change to pay for the pie and coffee. (Country Cousins Restaurant only accepted Canadian money.)

Saturday night after the board meeting Steve took me to another prairie town called Carbon. Again this was a very small community with one restaurant called "Plain and Fancy." This restaurant was noted for its delicious buffet and homemade desserts. We were met at the door by the owner. He was from Germany and had a strong accent. He asked if we had reservations to which we said: "No!" He continued by saying that was too bad because he had no open tables. Besides he began to tell us we would miss out on halupkies, pierogies and some other German dishes. Since he had all those items, I asked: "Did he have garage keys"? He said he didn't know what they were. I responded that they were the keys to open the garage door. He began to laugh and said come with me. We went toward the kitchen and he called out to his wife. "Anna, Anna, listen what this man just asked me." He had me tell her what I had just asked him. He began to laugh hardily again and turned toward me saying, "I will make room for you even if I have to put you in the kitchen." Each year thereafter when I

176

went to Three Hills, Steve and I would make our way to Carbon and the Plain and Fancy Restaurant.

My annual trip to Three Hills fell into an established pattern. I usually had breakfast at the "Coffee Cup" in Three Hills. This was a local hangout for the ranchers and farmers of the area. Every morning there were rows and rows of pickup trucks whose owners were inside having breakfast and talking about their things of interest. I would meet with the office staff, arrange for any interviews with prospective candidates, prepare for the annual board meeting and check out the map for the church where I would be speaking the following Sunday. There was always time for Steve and I to take a short drive to Lake Louise and Banff.

Lake Louise is a tourist attraction that attracts thousands of tourists every year. It is located in Banff National Park in the Canadian Rockies adjacent to the Canadian Pacific Railroad. The short drive from Calgary to Lake Louise was always a real treat to me because of the beauty of the Rockies and the opportunity to see herds of elk, mountain goats and, at least once, a cow moose. On one of our trips we came across the destruction left by an avalanche that occurred a few days before. The destruction was severe and very hard to describe. It uprooted large trees dragging them down the mountainside while picking up stones and gravel. The debris covered the entire highway and large earth moving equipment had to be called in to clear the road.

When we arrived at Lake Louise we parked across the road from the Fairmount Chateau. On one side of the entrance to the parking lot were several inches of snow while on the other side the roadway was clear. The mission Board Meetings were always held in April. The nights were well below freezing with only a few degrees warmer during the afternoon. You could always see areas of snow on the ground on the trip from Calgary to Banff. The Fairmount Chateau is a luxury hotel built in 1890. It is a large accommodation with 548 rooms with all the modern conveniences. Steve and I would walk through the main lobby and past some of the gift shops. On one of our trips I saw a beautiful ring at one of the gift shops and bought it for Elaine. That was all that I bought at this luxurious hotel because the prices were out of my budget.

On one of my trips to attend the Canadian board meeting, Steve informed me that he had received an application from someone in Edmonton. And he arranged for us to drive there to interview the candidate. It would take us several hours to drive to Edmonton so we stared the trip early in the morning in order to be ready to interview the candidate before lunch. We had a good trip discussing mission business and taking in the wonderful scenery that Canada has to offer.

The interview went well and after lunch with the candidate I thought we would start our trip back to Three Hills. Instead Steve said he had a surprise for me. We would first tour one of the world's largest shopping malls. I couldn't believe how large the area the mall filled. I know now that we didn't see it in its entirety, but what I saw intrigued me. There was an ice skating rink, a wave swimming pool, miles and miles of shops, scores of all kinds of eating places and the most interesting display of several classic cars in a roped-off area. I saw a 1949 Mercury sedan as if it came out of the factory marked with a sale price of $1,800 and a 1948 Oldsmobile convertible listed at $850, just to mention a few. I talked with the individual who was in charge of the display to learn that those prices were the prices when they were on the showroom floor of the car dealer, not what they could be purchased for now. I was thinking if they could be bought for those prices now how would I arrange financing to at least purchase one, even if I had to drive it back home. Hearing his answer to my question took care of any plans that had begun to form in my mind. Walking back to where we entered the center we stopped for a quick bite to eat and watch a television commercial being shot a short distance away. It was quite a full day.

During the ten years that I traveled to attend the board meetings I had the privilege of speaking in several churches. I enjoyed meeting the pastors and talking with them about their ministry and the scope of FIM's missionary outreach around the world.

FIM Board of
Directors meeting,
USA

FIM full Board, USA

FIM Board, Canada

179

Lake Louise

Avalanche in Alberta

# FIM Travel

My main objective as Executive Director was to personally visit as many of our missionaries as I had the opportunity to do either when they were in the States or on their field of ministry. Prior to my taking office, missionaries home on furlough were expected to come to the office to report to the Board of Directors. It was an informal meeting with the missionary reviewing their ministry of the past four years. There was time for questions and answers and always the guarantee that the board was fully behind them to help in any way possible. I found that some of the missionaries had come home on furlough but had never informed the office of their plans. I received several phone calls from pastors informing me that the missionary and his family had been home for a few months without our knowledge. I began contacting missionaries who were home on furlough and arranged for me to meet them while they were in the States. My plan was to inform them of our new office procedures and to notify them of their responsibilities to the home office. In my personal meeting with them I would stress the importance of their monthly reports. It was from them that we were made aware of any problems or needs. We would use information from their reports to add to the prayer prompter that was sent out with the receipts to all supporters. This would provide a broad prayer base for our missionary family. Every missionary had already received information from the Board of Directors announcing my responsibility with the mission and some of the goals to be advanced in the days ahead. I was convinced that if we were to move the mission forward changes had to be made. The best way to put them into practice was for me to meet with them face-to-face. This meant that I would need to travel from time to time to accomplish this goal.

## Brazil

I had my first introduction to travel to meet with missionaries in 1982. While a member of the Board of Directors an invitation was received by Paul Platt for someone to visit with them. Bill Simpkins, the Board

President, agreed to go but they wanted another board member to accompany him. They asked if I would be willing to join Bill and travel to be with FIM missionaries in Brazil. I received permission from my board of elders. The assistant pastor was to oversee the ministry of First Baptist Church until I returned. The date of our arrival was suggested by the missionaries and as we checked our calendars it didn't give us much time to get all our necessary paperwork in order. Bill and my passports were still active but we needed visas to enter the country. Bill and I drove to Jersey City to take the subway into Manhattan where the Brazilian Embassy was located. I was surprised at the courtesy of the clerk who took our information. She said she could have our visas ready in a few hours and that we could pick them up before their office closed at 5:00 pm. Bill and I took a subway down town to Chinatown and had a bite to eat. When we returned to the Brazilian Embassy our visas were ready. Bill and I walked around Times Square before taking the PATH train back to Jersey City to get our car and drive back home.

Time for our trip soon arrived and Bill and I were driven to Kennedy airport by one of Bill's parishioners. Our plane left Kennedy at about 7:00 pm. The plane was not full, so some of the passengers took the center section and used the seats as a bed because we would be flying most of the night. Upon our arrival at Sao Paulo, Brazil we were met by Skip Harkins and his son. Skip and his son took us to see Earl and Joann Metz. Earl was building a church building in Sao Paulo. They prepared a Brazilian lunch for us. After spending a few hours with the Metz family, Skip Harkins drove us to their home in Atibaia. They had been doing some work on their car and didn't have time to replace the shock absorbers which made our ride quite uncomfortable. We were with the Harkins for some time learning about their ministry. We spent our first night with the Harkins. The next morning they took us to the other side of town to see Marcos Souza and his family. The Souza's were a musical family and were involved with not only traveling around Brazil giving sacred concerts but they also had established a camp ministry which included a soccer camp. They would host several weeks of youth camp with emphasis on soccer. Soccer was very popular in Brazil and it was easier for them to get campers because they emphasized soccer. They always would include a musical concert and give a gospel message to the campers.

The next day Skip drove us back to Sao Paulo airport to fly to Londrina. Paul Guiley met us at the airport and drove us to his home. Paul and Viola Guiley came to Londrina several years ago and established Maranatha Bible Institute where they trained students for the pastorate or missions work. Paul had arranged a very active schedule for us while visiting with him. I found that Viola had a good sense of humor and I enjoyed kidding around with her and her with me. It made our stay with them quite enjoyable. Bill and I toured the dormitories and spent some time with the students. Bill was asked to address the student body. I believe we spent about a day or two with the students before we accompanied Paul on a trip to tour some of the churches that the graduates had established. We started out on a sunny day. At lunch time we stopped at a truck stop on the Pan-American Highway. The three of us had a Brazilian buffet type dinner called a churrascaria. It was quite an experience. The waiter would bring a spit of barbecued meat to the table and we would tell him how much to cut off. I didn't speak Portuguese and the waiter didn't understand English so I just grunted and he sliced off a piece of meat onto my plate.

We visited several of the young churches that were started by the graduates of Maranatha Bible Institute. We were in Brazil during part of the rainy season. One day as we were driving on this rain soaked, gravel road we drove into a hole and got stuck. Bill and I without any umbrella went out of the car to view the situation. I told Bill that I believed I could push the car backwards and if we got enough stones to fill the hole, we might be able to get going again. I started to find large stones and threw them to Bill who remained at the front of the car. Paul Guiley's car was a small Chevy produced in Brazil. When you opened the hood all you saw was a small motor, a radiator and a battery. After a few minutes of throwing the large stones I began to push the light car back as far as I could and Bill threw the rocks into the hole. This too was no use. We were soaked and covered with Brazil's red mud. At last a large bus came to our aid and with a tow rope he was able to pull us out of the hole. A few miles away we

183

stopped at a gas station, took out the floor mats and hosed out the red mud. When I got home and Elaine tried to wash out the red mud, it was useless and the pants had to be thrown away.

Paul saved the best to the last. It was the last day to spend with him and he wanted us to see one of the unusual sites of Brazil. We drove to the Foz do Iguaçu. This city is right next to the Iguazu Falls. These are gigantic water falls that actually join three countries together. They are located at the southwestern tip of Brazil next to Paraguay and Argentina. These falls make Niagara Falls look very small in comparison. The lip of the falls are approximately 2 miles across. Because of the distance we needed to travel to return to Maratha Bible Institute, we made arrangements to stay in a motel in Brazil. After a delicious meal we rented a cab and the driver drove us into Paraguay. This way we could visit the city without getting a visa. We walked around the town that was buzzing with activity. Street vendors and street preachers were everywhere. After a couple of hours we took the cab back to our motel.

Our next city to visit was Aracatuba. It was quite a distance from the Bible Institute so we traveled by bus. We took the night sleeper from Londrina to Aracatuba. The trip would take us all night. The bus was a luxury liner with comfortable reclining seats. As soon as we got started the person in front of me fully reclined his seat and pinned my knees tight against the back of his seat. The rest of the ride was not very comfortable.

Bill and I arrived in Aracatuba the next morning and were met by George Harman. George's mother and father had been in Brazil for many years. Over their tenure three children were born into their family. All three were now grown and all working with their mates in Aracatuba. They had established a large Bible Church and Bible Institute. The students in the Bible Institute would hold Sunday school classes every Sunday afternoon around Aracatuba wherever they could find shade. Some classes were held in homes, garages and under trees. The Sunday we were at the Bible Church, they had set a goal to have 2,000 attending all the Sunday school classes in the church and outside around the city. When the final count was given the attendance was over 2,000. George and Eunice his wife had formed a soccer camp and invited teens from around Brazil to attend. The camp was well organized and young people heard the gospel message. John and his wife were very much involved in the Bible Church. The senior Harman's were elderly and not in good health. The senior Mr. Harman had a stroke and was not able to speak. His wife had polio many years ago and was confined to a wheelchair. Despite her handicap, she taught Christian Education at the Bible Institute. Joy and her husband taught in the Bible Institute.

When I was asked to join Bill on this trip Elaine wasn't sure if it was a good idea for me to leave the country. Brazil is a long distance from Pennsylvania. She said she would give me her blessing if I would bring back some jewelry. Before I left Paul Guiley, he introduced me to a local businessman who had some Brazilian cut stones and was willing to sell them for American dollars. I won't go into what took place in his office but I came home with a small leather bag filled with sparkling Brazilian stones and two small rubies. I had some of the stones made into rings for Elaine, Roxann, my mother-in-law, daughter-in-law and my step-mother. For the men I had tie tacks made. I had a tremendous time and my interest in missions was multiplied a hundred-fold.

# Morocco

In 1988, I was again asked to accompany Bill on another mission's trip. This time it was to Morocco. We flew from Kennedy International Airport in New York to Casablanca. We arrived early in the morning and were met by Jim Pitts. Jim Pitts was the director of The Children's Haven located in Azrou some distance from the airport.

The Children's Haven was started by Mary Mellinger and Irene Wenzhold. They went to Morocco to begin working with women but before long a woman came to their home with a child that she no longer could care for. This was the beginning of the Children's Haven ministry. It has been in existence since 1950. These two ladies formed the Moroccan Evangelical Mission and it continued to exist under that name for several years. A Board of Directors was formed and York Gospel Tabernacle served as its headquarters. A few years later Frank Baggott and his family were approached by one of the board members to become associated with the Moroccan Evangelical Mission. Frank Baggott, his wife Idabel, his son Steven and his daughter Mary founded the Sahara Desert Mission. Their mission board was based in England. It was the joining of the two independent mission agencies that gave birth to a new name of Fellowship of Independent Missions.

The Children's Haven grew with the addition of more children. New missionaries joined the team at the Children's Haven and new buildings were erected to meet the need. The children were cared for by the missionaries and treated as if they were their own. An elementary school was established and later a junior high and senior high school were added. When the children reached the age of eighteen they moved out of the Children's Haven to find work in the surrounding cities. Some of the students after graduation went under sponsorship to the U.S. for further college training.

Bill and I were at the Haven to celebrate the graduation exercise. We stayed in one of the guest rooms. The first night my sleep was disturbed about five o'clock in the morning by a mule heehawing every few minutes. I also had some indigestion from the supper we had the night before. We were introduced to Moroccan cooking by being served Tagine. Tagine was served in a metal dish similar to a cake pan. There were several small round meatballs in a tomato sauce. You would take a piece of Moroccan bread and use it like a spoon to pick up a meat ball and some sauce. We also had a dish of couscous which looked like fine rice. It was served in a large dish with one half dry and the other half moist with a thin gravy. Again you used some Moroccan bread to serve as a spoon to take either from the dry side or the moist side. Everyone around the table would take turns spooning from either side.

186

We were able to see the sites in Casablanca, Meknes, Fez, Rabat and a tour of the open market in Azrou. Jim Pitts had been at the Haven for many years and had become friendly with many of the vendors at the market. Jim was able to talk freely with them in Arabic. Most of the meat and produce was purchased at the market.

Upon leaving the Haven we traveled to Casablanca to board our plane for the flight back home. Before I boarded the plane I needed to use the restroom. What a mistake that was. The restroom hadn't been cleaned for what looked like a month or two. I suddenly realized after taking a few steps into the room that I really could wait until I boarded the plane and use a clean restroom. The flight back to the States was a smooth flight. It was good to be back home but happy that I had the opportunity to see FIM's first missionary endeavor.

Bill and Ruth Simpkins          Harkins family

Earl & Joanne Metz

Marcos Souza
and family

188

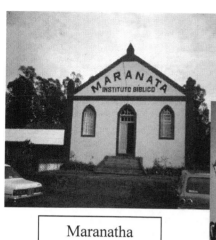

Maranatha
Bible Institute

Paul & Viola
Guiley

Stuck in Brazil's red mud

189

Foz do Iquacu

George &
Eunice Harmon

Senior Harmons

Children's Haven family with Mary Mellinger

Me with 1988 graduating class

Children's Haven, Azrou, Morocco

# Flexibility, Integrity, Accountability

Now that FIM had its own facilities, a procedures and policy manual and a candidate school, we were ready to continue to build to become a bona fide mission agency and to outlive our old reputation of being a clearing house for funds. We were becoming more visible by representing FIM at Bible Schools and Seminaries. By cooperating in mission's conferences in those institutions of higher learning and in local churches, we began to have more interested people requesting information about FIM. Every June we saw an average of 10 new candidates enrolled in the candidate school. There was one year when several candidates weren't able to get their paper work in on time so they postponed their applications until the following year.

My schedule was full with overseeing the day-to-day operations and speaking in missionary conferences and churches on behalf of the mission. While driving on one of my trips to be with our missionaries in Battle Creek, MI, I was thinking about a phrase that could serve as a foundation platform of the philosophy of FIM. I came up with this motto: Flexibility in Ministry with Integrity and Accountability. At our next board meeting I introduced this motto and the Board unanimously agreed that it was to be the motto to build upon.

Flexibility meant that we as an agency would not place a missionary in a ministry of our choosing. We would honor the ministry desire of the missionary candidate as long as his or her supporting church agreed with their ministry plan.

Integrity meant that the missionary would serve with honesty and trustworthiness where ever he or she would serve.

Accountability meant the missionary would regularly communicate with their supporters and the home office. They would be faithful in submitting the required reports on time.

Some of our missionaries were nationals serving in their respected countries as FIM missionaries. In keeping with our vision and goal to have better communication with all of our missionary family, we needed to have these nationals come back to the States for ministry review and an opportunity to assist them in their respective ministries. They were having difficulty in securing the proper visas necessary for coming to the States. I wrote to the Immigration Department in Washington, DC, but received no answer or communication.

When serving as a board member for the Christian Servicemen's center in Aberdeen, MD, we had recently expanded this ministry to Aniston, AL. One of the board members that served with me at Aberdeen was Rev. Donald Balfour from South River, NJ. His son Donald Balfour Jr. became a board member at Aniston. At a joint board meeting I was introduced to Donald Jr. and learned that he was Senator Donald Balfour Jr. of Georgia. I told him of my problem with getting the national missionaries proper visas and the fact that I hit a brick wall with the immigration people. He told me he would see what he could do.

Several months passed when I received a phone call from Senator Balfour. He told me he had arranged a meeting with the Director of Immigration and I should plan to meet him in DC on January 3rd and be prepared to stay overnight because the next day we would meet with Newt Gingrich just prior to him being sworn in as the Speaker of the House. He told me to get a motel in Silver Springs, MD because the cost to stay in DC was quite high.

It was late on the afternoon of January 2nd, 1995, when I checked into a motel in Silver Springs, MD. I met Senator Balfour the next morning at his hotel in DC. We took a cab to the building that housed the Department of Immigration. After going through security we were ushered into the Director's office. He rose from his chair to greet us and offered us a seat. As I looked around his office, his walls were lined with large pictures of steam trains. I told him those pictures of the trains looked like the ones at Strasburg, PA. He said that they were those trains and that his hobby was trains. He asked me to follow him as he walked to the far end of his office where an old Lionel train was on display on a large table. It was exactly like the one I had at home except that mine was a little older. His Lionel train had automatic couplers where mine had the manual. When he heard that his eyes lit up and before he could say anything I immediately spoke up saying that he shouldn't get any ideas because my train was not for sale. That seemed to break the ice and he became very friendly. We returned to our seats and proceeded to review the problem of the visas. As he spoke I began taking notes. He stopped me and said he would give me all this information in writing for my record.

As we were preparing to leave he told me that if I had any questions that might come up in the future that I should fax the information to his secretary and he would address it. I thanked him and we went out of the building. Our meeting took the greater part of the afternoon. Senator Balfour returned to his hotel and I to the motel in Silver Springs. As we parted he reminded me that I needed to be at the steps of the Capital building the next morning at 8:00 am. He said that his mother and father and two businessmen would be there and all of us would go into the Capital building and meet Newt Gingrich. His parents were old friends of mine and I was anxious to see them again. I would meet the two businessmen there also. I rode the Metro System back to a station near the motel. The subway cars seemed a little larger and more spacious and cleaner than the New York or Philadelphia subway cars.

I arrived early the next morning and began to walk around the Capital building taking in the sights. On one of the corners was a coffee shop. Since I had plenty of time until I was to meet them, I stopped to get a cup of coffee and took it outside sipping as I walked around taking in everything that was going on around the Capital.

At 8:00 am I met Senator Balfour, his parents and two businessmen from Atlanta, GA who were personal friends of the Senator. The businessmen were a father and his son-in-law who together ran a gas station and a dry-cleaning business. We all followed the Senator into the Capital building to a large room. I estimated that there were well over a hundred people in the room. Over on one wall was a table filled with all kinds of pastries and coffee. After about an hour we were ushered into another room and introduced to Newt. We shook hands, spoke for a few minutes and posed for a picture with him. Later that afternoon his actual swearing in ceremony would take place.

Senator Balfour took all of us on a tour of the Capital building including a ride on the Underground Railroad that was used by the government officials. I don't know how many Senators and Congressman we passed on our tour but there were many familiar faces that I had seen at one time or another on TV or in the newspaper. It was quite an experience. For lunch we walked several blocks from the Capital building to the National Republican Club dining room. Quite impressive! In fact I still have a table placemat with their logo. Senator Balfour introduced us to Bert Rizzo, the Director of Congressional Affairs, Congressman John Linder of Georgia and Senator Paul Coverdale of Georgia. These men were seated near our table and greeted us warmly.

After lunch we all walked back to the Capital building hoping to be able to get a seat and witness the swearing in of Newt Gingrich. To our amazement the room was filled to capacity and people were actually sitting on the steps in the balcony. Senator Balfour decided to take us to Congressman John Linder's office to watch the proceeding on closed circuit TV.

The congressman welcomed us and had more chairs brought into his office for all of us. I sat next to the Congressmen's wife who offered all of us peanuts and Coke. There was an ample supply on hand because these items came from Georgia. Part way through the ceremony, the Congressman's wife excused herself. She said she thought things were too boring and wanted to go shopping.

After the ceremony was completed, we all said our goodbyes and went our separate ways. For me it was a very exciting day and one that will long remain in my memory. As we were leaving Senator Balfour handed me a ticket to attend the 104th Congressional Celebration. He asked me to join him that evening in one of the large ballrooms. He wanted just to make his appearance, greet some people and leave. He asked me to join him; we would come and leave together. It was quite an experience to mingle with all of those dignitaries. I certainly didn't fit in with that group. I kept the ticket that cost $25.00 to enter the ballroom and now have it in my file on the trip to Washington, DC.

About two months after my trip to Washington, DC, a large box came in the mail for me at the Mission office. As I opened the box I saw it was a large picture of our group that met with Newt Gingrich. At the bottom of the picture frame was a rectangular gold plaque with the following inscription: Newt Gingrich Speaker of the House, January 4th, 1995. Right below that plate was another white plaque with these words: "To Dick from your friend Newt." I hung that picture in my office and everyone who saw it made some kind of remark to which I answered: "We don't mess around here; we go right to the top."

Over the ten years that I served as General Director I had the opportunity and privilege of personally visiting with many of our missionary families as well as spending time with them when they were home on furlough either at their place of residence or in our office.

Republican Club
luncheon placemat

Senator Donald
Balfour Jr. and me

104th
Congressional
Celebration

Our gang with
Newt Gingrich

# Visiting Foreign Lands

I'd like to list the counties and the cities in those countries that I had visited and include some of the things that took place during my short visits.

## Brazil

### Sao Paulo

Sao Paulo looked like New York City with tall modern buildings, shopping areas, restaurants, busy streets and large crowds of people walking on the sidewalks. Some of the sidewalks were constructed like a checkerboard with alternating colors of black and white. As we drove through the city, the other end of town was a different sight. People were living under the underpasses of the highway system. They had made their homes out of old cardboard boxes, pieces of discarded lumber, old doors or whatever they could find. Farther on in the same section of the city were rows and rows of poorly constructed shacks. This was quite a contrast to the center of the city. I enjoyed my visit with Earl and Joann Metz.

### Capinas

Francisco DeSouza and his family made Capinas their home. Francisco opened a counselling center and pastored a small Brazilian church. We toured the small city and he pointed out places of interest. We passed the Brazilian army base and saw the soldiers marching and going through their routine. It began to rain and Francisco turned on his wipers but after one wipe they quit. He was embarrassed and said that his car was old and had some problems. I enjoyed my visit with the DeSouza family.

## Barganca

Itamar Santos conducted an after-school Bible club and summer camp ministries. He is very talented in art and used it in his classes. Barganca was a medium sized city with all the modern conveniences. Itamar lived on the fourth floor of a tall townhouse building. We walked from his apartment to the school which was only a few blocks away. Barganca is a very hilly city on the order of San Francisco. I had to walk cautiously because the cobblestone sidewalks were slippery with my leather soled shoes. The students were happy to see us and treated us warmly.

## Londrina

Londrina was a small town where Paul and Viola Guiley established a Bible Institute to train pastors and missionaries in a three-year program. Paul introduced me to the student body and took me on a tour of the facilities. That evening the students sang and we had a short church service. This was my second visit to Maranatha Bible Institute. My first was in 1982 with Bill Simpkins, President of the Board of Directors of FIM. I visited again ten years later. My purpose of this second trip was to sit in on a meeting with Paul and several area pastors who were interested in taking over the Bible Institute and all of its property. Paul was now in his mid-80s and Viola was recovering from a stroke. It was time to make a change in their ministry and Paul wanted me there for my opinion of the plan the other pastors were going to present. Since I don't know Portuguese I had invited Earl Metz, our missionary in Sao Paulo, to accompany me on this trip and serve as my interpreter. We almost didn't make this trip together because a short time before I arrived in Brazil to meet up with Earl, he had been doing some work on his car. The car was jacked up in the front and he was underneath working on the problem when the jack slipped and the some of the car rested on his shoulder. He was fortunate that nothing more serious happened and he could accompany me on this trip.

I listened to Earl translate what the pastors were presenting to Paul and what they intended to do with the Institute. After the meeting was over only Paul, Earl and I remained in Paul's office. Paul asked me for my opinion. I explained my thoughts and suggested that what the pastors wanted to do would be a detriment to the school and its philosophy of Christian instruction. He thanked me and we all went to Paul's house for the evening meal. Most Brazilian meals included black beans, white rice, some type of meat and cafezinaho or guarana. Cafezinaho was a strong Brazilian sweet coffee usually served in small demitasse cups. I really enjoyed the coffee and drank it every chance it was offered. Guarana is a carbonated fruit drink very popular in Brazil. I also enjoyed that drink as well and always took a glass of the drink when offered.

After the evening meal was over we all sat in Paul's living room making plans for our departure the next morning. Before we retired for the night, Viola served us some puffy pastries and a coke. On my previous visit to the Guiley's I found out that Viola was quite a kidder. I had played some tricks on her on that visit but this time I behaved myself thinking of her health. She may have had some setback physically because of the stroke but her sense of humor was still there. She served me the tray of pastries and turned the tray so that the first row was in front of me. She told me to take the first two, which I did. After serving the others we began to bite into the pastries. I took my first bite but couldn't bite completely through. I tried again with the same results. I watched the others enjoying their treat but I didn't look at Viola purposely. I took one more attempt and pulled hard on the dough. I was successful and I found that the center was filled with cotton. I looked over at Viola and she was laughing hilariously and said "Ha, Ha, I got you back." The next morning when we said our goodbyes we both had tears in our eyes.

## *Aracatuba*

Earl Metz and I traveled to Aracatuba. This was also my second trip to this city. The Harman family continued to do various types of ministries. The Bible Church, the Bible Institute, Christian day school, sports camp and radio ministry.

## Reo Petro

Alden and Virginia Barrows had established a church here and were involved with a building program when we arrived. We arrived during the week and did not have a chance to visit when a church service was being conducted. Virginia was recuperating from a car crash that demolished their van. They were travelling on the Pan American Highway which is only two lanes wide. They were going down a hill and another vehicle was going up the hill in the opposite direction traveling very slowly behind an over weighted truck. The driver of the slower vehicle grew impatient, pulled out to pass the truck over a double line and hit their car head-on. They were very thankful that neither of them was killed.

## Goiana

John and Anna Harmon moved from Aracatuba to begin a new ministry here. They started a church and began a Bible Institute. I spoke at their church and at the Bible Institute. After the Sunday night service we were all standing outside the church building talking when two of the church members came up to me with a large glass bowl filled with what looked like large black grapes. They were husband and wife and both were dentists. They were present for the evening service but left after the service and went home. They lived a short distance from the church so they could return quickly with the bowl of Brazilian fruit. They said something to me in Portuguese and John Harman served as my interpreter. They wanted to know if I wanted some jabuticaba. John explained to me that it was a large thick-skinned grape similar to what we would find here growing on backyard grapevines. I took one up in my hands and squeezed the meat into my mouth and threw the skin on the ground. It was delicious. I thanked them and began eating more, throwing the skins on the ground. Others joined in and when the bowl was empty the street was covered with the skins from the jabuticaba.

Before I left Goiana John showed me another kind of a Brazilian fruit that everyone enjoyed. It looked like a squash with pimples. I did not taste it but said to John that I thought the Portuguese language was strange to me. I said that when he told me the name of the small grape like fruit and called it jabuticaba and then showed me a larger squash like fruit and call it jaca that the language to me was confusing. A small fruit had a big name and a big fruit had a little name. This to me was most confusing to say the least.

## *Atibaia*

We also spent a day with Marcos Souza and his family. Marcos was a Brazilian Indian from the north of Brazil. Marcos was born into a poor Indian family in Matogrosso. A single lady who was a missionary working with Word of Life became very fond of Marcos and after a period of time, because of the family's dire situation, she received permission from his parents to adopt him as her son. She had an old-fashioned pump organ that Marcos learned to play. Later he mastered the guitar. He enrolled at the Word of Life Bile Institute in Atibaia and sharpened his musical skills. He later met a young lady who had been a lawyer and they soon married. Over the years the Lord blessed them with several children all of whom became very musical. They used their musical talents to give Christian concerts all over Brazil. In the summer months they hosted soccer camps and presented the gospel through music and preaching.

Skip Harkins and his family had started a church on the other side of town. That night I was to preach at that church but first Skip wanted me to see their summer campsite across the lake near their home. To get there we had to take his homemade boat. I wouldn't have believed it if I hadn't actually seen it. It was a couple of 50-gallon steel barrels welded together to form the hull of the boat. Skip had rigged up an outboard motor with an exposed engine. I got into the boat and noticed alongside of the boat we were towing a homemade barge loaded with chicken feed and some other items needed at the campsite. Skip's son Kenny was at the controls and we started across the lake. About halfway across the motor began to sputter but neither Kenny nor Skip paid much attention to it. So I called it to Kenny's attention and he simply reached down to the carburetor and adjusted the needle valve setting. The motor again began to run smoothly. The Harkins family is very adept in making practical things out of things that were discarded by other people as junk. The boat was an example and when we docked the boat on the island, I saw another example of their handiwork. They had rigged up a pumping system drawing water from the lake to irrigate some of the crops they had planted for use during the camping season. On the way back across the lake it began to rain. I was wondering if that would affect the attendance since most of the church members walked to church. As the service was about to begin; the people came, their coats wet and smelly, but they came. The small room was filled with people. Marcos and his family came to provide the music. Marcos approached me and wanted me to sing a solo. I really wasn't willing to do it but they all insisted. That was the first and last solo I sang.

# Sweden

## *Stockholm*

I was invited to serve on the advisory board along with several other Mission Executives at their annual meeting which was always held in December. December in Sweden meant that we would only have a few hours of daylight. By three o'clock in the afternoon it started to get dark. Several of our missionaries serving in Sweden began using friendship evangelism to start churches. They lived in townhouses and would invite their neighbors for meals or desserts. Eventually they would have a Bible study. As the group grew they would hold a church service in the community hall in the basement of the building. While I was there I was invited to speak to the church as they met in the community hall. The hall was beautifully decorated because it was used for many different gatherings. This particular Sunday I preached in English, a person interpreted my message into Swedish. In front of me a small group of people sat in a circle and the Swedish words were interpreted into Arabic. That morning three people invited Christ to be their Saviour.

## *Garbo*

John and Judy Breneman have been in Sweden for many years. John teaches counselling at a Bible Institute and has established a counselling center in Stockholm. I spent several days with John and Judy. On one occasion John invited me to accompany him to Stockholm because he had a counselling session that day. We took the bus to Stockholm and arrived at lunch time. As we began walking down the street he informed me that I would be on my own for lunch. It came as a surprise because I had no idea what was good Swedish food or not good and besides I didn't have any Swedish money. John was very helpful. His suggestion was for me to walk across the street to the bank and exchange some American dollars for Swedish dollars. After I received the exchange I started to walk up the street looking for places to eat. Stockholm is a very large city and reminded me of Philadelphia or New York City. I looked at the menus posted on the windows. I couldn't believe the prices. I wasn't prepared to pay a high price for lunch since I only had a few Swedish dollars, and the amount of American dollars in my pocket was running quite low. I saw a McDonald's a block away but I didn't come to Sweden to eat McDonald's. However, after walking for what seemed to be forever and looking for a reasonable place to eat, I settled on Pizza Hut and had spaghetti at the cost of $12.00.

After John's session we took the bus back home. After supper John asked me to go with him to the home of one of the Board members who served on the Board of Directors of the counseling center. The board member was a doctor and his wife a nurse. When you enter a home in Sweden you remove your shoes. Since it was December and there was snow on the ground I removed my shoes and walked into their living room. After I was introduced I took a seat. John and the Doctor began to talk about the counseling center. The phone rang and the Doctor took the message. He excused himself and had to leave to attend to an emergency. After he left the Doctor's wife invited us to come into the kitchen for some coffee and dessert. I began to leave the living room and walk to the kitchen. The floor of the kitchen was about an inch higher than the floor in the living room. As I raised my foot to step into the kitchen I didn't raise it high enough and stubbed my toe on the lip of the kitchen floor. I had hit it with enough force that it threw me off balance and I fell onto the kitchen floor. The Doctor's wife ran over to me shouting, "Are you hurt? Are you hurt?" My answer was simply; "No, only my pride is hurt." I really felt embarrassed.

My toe really did hurt. When I got back to John's house I was glad to take off my shoes because I was in pain. My bed was John and Judy's sofa. I spent a restless night with the pain in my toe. The next day I found it very painful to put on my shoe. That day we did a great deal of walking. That night when I took off my shoes and socks I saw my toe had turned black. Now I know what a broken toe feels like.

## *Uppsala & Goteborg*

I concluded my trip to Sweden with a short trip to Uppsala and Goteborg. Uppsala has a large student population attending the university. Goteborg is a large modern city. I stayed with Doug and Ann Jackson for a short time. Doug took me to a museum and I saw an original Viking ship that had been rescued from the sea after it sank. It was very interesting to move around the ship wondering what it must have been like during a sea battle. We took a tour of the city of Goteborg which reminded me of Philadelphia or New York City. It was while I was visiting with the Jacksons that they received word that a colleague had suddenly passed away. The Jacksons began to make arrangements to attend the funeral some distance from Goteborg.

Doug Jackson and John Breneman had come to Sweden to work with Ed Fuchs. All of tham had been graduates from Dallas Theological Seminary. After Ed graduated from Dallas he came to Sweden to start a Bible College. One of the young men, Gosta Eriksson, was recruited by Ed and sent to Dallas Seminary. When he had completed his schooling he returned to Sweden to work with Ed, Doug and John teaching at the Bible College. Gosta had contracted a rare disease and quite suddenly had passed away. It was Gosta's funeral that the Jacksons and Brenemans were making arrangements to attend. I was invited to attend with the Jacksons.

The funeral service was held in Saffle some distance north of Goteborg in an old Swedish church. The exterior was constructed of stone with Swedish exterior wooden trim. As you enter the sanctuary all the fixtures were very old. There was an aisle in the middle of the sanctuary that separated the pews on either side. In order to enter a pew, you would have to open a small door and step up one step. They used bricks that they warmed to keep your feet warm during the service. The entire service was in Swedish and even though I didn't understand one word, the spirit of the service was very reverent and respectful. As I write the description of the funeral even after all those years that have passed, the memory is very clear and still impresses me.

# Australia

## *Melbourne & Warragul*

Warragul was several miles from Melbourne and the town where Dick and Ree Andes lived. Dick had recently recovered from a stroke and had just passed his driver's test. When he suffered the stroke he had to give up his driver's license. Dick liked to play golf and was permitted to equip an ATV with a basket welded to the back of it to carry his golf clubs. The owner of the course allowed Dick to drive the ATV but he could not exceed 1st gear.

Dick and Ree had established a camp program and were expanding to the establishment of a Bible Institute. The camp was well established with many activities for the campers to enjoy. Dick made a water slide out of long strips of rubber that began high on a hill and extended down the grade for over a city block. He would run water from the top which ran all the way to the bottom. The campers would start at the top and the water would allow them to slide all the way to the bottom picking up speed as they traveled down the slide.

## Brisbane & Toowoomba

I stayed in Toowoomba where Arthur and Dorothy Johns lived. Arthur had been involved in an automobile accident a short time before my arrival and was confined to a wheelchair. It was not known for sure if he would ever be able to walk again. A special van was built for Arthur that gave him easy access and made it possible for him to accompany his family when traveling. They were a wonderful host and hostess taking the time to show me many of the sights of their hometown and even travel to Brisbane to take in the sights of the beautiful beaches and the Pacific Ocean. Their ministry consisted of conducting several home Bible studies.

## Sydney

FIM had two women missionaries, Marilyn Hutchison and Linda Hochman, who conducted after school Bible clubs in several elementary schools. My first night in Sydney I attended a board meeting with the two missionaries as they shared their ministry with their board members. I was introduced to an older couple who served on their board for a long time. My first impression of this couple was that they seemed to be quite stern and a couple of stuffed shirts. When the meeting was over I was told that this couple would be my host and hostess while I stayed in Sydney. The two missionaries would be busy the next day with some other activities and I would be on my own. I thought it to be odd since they knew of my coming long in advance that they could not have made better arrangements. But what would be would be.

My host and hostess took me home in their car. What a ride. The man was blind in one eye and his wife had to tell him if traffic was coming on his blind side. I thought that I would be in for a rather boring time with this couple. When we arrived at their apartment they showed me to the guest bedroom and bath. I don't remember their names but my host asked me what my plans were for the next day. I told him I would take a train into Sydney and take in the sights. He smiled at me and said, "Young man, my wife and I will be your guide." I certainly wasn't expecting this and wasn't sure what kind of a day I would have with these stuffed shirts. Before he said goodnight he told me that at 7:00 am he always prepared a cup of tea and a biscuit for his wife and brought them to her in their bedroom. He asked if I would also like the same. I told him that I would certainly appreciate that.

The next morning at 7:00 am there was a knock on my door and he presented me with a cup of tea and a biscuit (to an American it was a cookie). After breakfast we all made our way to the train station. We purchased our tickets and he told me that this ticket would not only be used for our train ride round trip but it would also be able to be used to ride a bus.

This really was turning out to be a great day. Those two were a lot of fun. I had misjudged them. They took me places that I would not have seen without them. Unbeknown to me they had planned to do this when they found out I was coming to visit the two missionaries. We took several bus rides to see various sights of the city using the same ticket we purchased at the train station that morning. The highlight of my trip to Sydney was to see the Opera House. It certainly turned out to be a terrific day.

The next day I spent with the two women missionaries while they conducted an after-school Bible club meeting at a nearby school. Later I went to a zoo like park and was able to hold a koala bear. They have very sharp claws so the zoo attendant placed the koala on a fur lined piece of bark and handed the koala to me to hold.

What I thought would be a dull adventure in Sydney turned out to be one of my best adventures.

# Japan

## *Nagoya, Toyohashi & Osaka*

Osaka and Nagoya were two large cities where air travelers had the option to enter the country. I was requested to land at Nagoya where Takuji Yamazaki met me at the airport. I went through customs and walked out into a sea of Japanese faces, bright lights and a TV camera crew. Immediately I thought, what a terrific welcome to Japan.

When my eyes became accustomed to the brightness I saw the camera crew pointing their cameras at a Japanese model posing at a large display of apples that had been shipped from the State of Washington.

Takuji had brought with him one of the men from his church. His name was Mr. Yamamoto. Mr. Yamamoto could not speak any English and I couldn't speak any Japanese. Takuji had been educated in the States and became my interpreter. We drove for several hours to get to Takauji's home in Toyohashi. We travelled on a modern highway but every couple of miles we had to stop to pay a toll. It was later in the day when we arrived at Toyohashi. Takuji had established the Grace Bible Church of Toyohashi. Takuji's wife Hiroko and their two girls lived on the second floor above the church. The girls would have an early morning breakfast, put on their backpacks, hop on their bicycles and pedal to the railroad station where they would take the train to the school they were attending. It would be dark when they would return home after their day at school. In the evening after they had their evening meal, they would practice their musical instruments and do their homework. This became their daily routine.

Mr. Yamamoto came to Takauji's house where I was staying and the three of us went on a sightseeing trip of Toyohashi. The Toyota's are built here. Toyohashi is a very large city with a population of 373,000 people seemingly crammed into a small area. The congregation of Grace Bible Church had purchased land high on a hill overlooking the city to use as a cemetery. The Japanese people had their own burial practices. The Christians attending Grace Bible Church wanted their burial procedures to be more in line with the Bible.

The city streets were jammed with people similar to New York City. As we drove around the city I couldn't help but notice many buildings with bright decorative lights flashing off and on. I was told they were Pachinko's. These were gambling facilities that were extremely popular with the Japanese.

Mr. Yamamoto and I began communicating using sign language. His favorite thing was to play a joke on me every chance he could. For example, I gave Mr. Yamamoto our mission prayer card with Elaine's and my picture on the front. He would take it out of his wallet; place his thumb over my face so that only Elaine's picture was visible. He would waive the picture at me, smiling as he did it.

That night Mr. Yamamoto joined us for the evening meal. Hiroko prepared the meal and it was authentic Japanese cooking. She placed a small bowl next to my plate and put a raw egg next to the small bowl. Next she placed a large bowl with steaming vegetables and pieces of beef. I watched to see what would happen next. Everyone took the raw egg and cracked it placing the raw egg into the small bowl. Next with the chopsticks they took some vegetables and mixed them with the raw egg. The heat of the vegetables caused the egg to cook and produce a thin coating that covered the piece of vegetable. They repeated the procedure with the meat. To my surprise following their procedure I found the vegetables and beef very tasty. This was authentic Japanese cooking.

After supper I wanted to walk several blocks away to a large grocery store and small mall. I was interested in seeing the prices of groceries. As we walked to the mall, Takuji, his one daughter and Mr. Yamamoto and I walked down a dark street when a dog began to bark. Mr. Yamamoto said something in Japanese that I did not understand. I didn't say anything to Takauji and kept on walking. After we had walked a few feet more I reached down and touched the back of Mr.

Yamasata's leg and barked like a dog. He jumped and shouted quite a long sentence in Japanese.

After walking through the grocery store we went into the mall and I offered to buy each of us an ice cream cone. We all had a small cone and the price was around $90.00.

The next Sunday Takuji took me to preach at a church started by a missionary where as a young man he had accepted Christ as his Saviour. As you enter the church you see small sandals lined up against the wall. You are to take off your shoes and slip into one of these pair of sandals. I looked at the row of sandals and didn't find one pair that would fit me. My feet were much bigger than the largest pair there. So I put on my bedroom slippers that I brought with me at the suggestion of Takuji.

After the service I was given an honorarium which I refused. However, Takuji told me to accept it because if I didn't it would offend them. I put the honorarium in my sport coat pocket. Upon leaving the church the American missionary that founded the church asked me if I played golf. I was prepared because on most of my trips I would always pack my golf shoes and some golf balls just in case I had an opportunity to play golf.

The American missionary picked me up the next morning after breakfast and took me to a newly opened golf course as his guest. While he was making the arrangements for us to begin the round, I stood under an overhang with open sides to video the golf course. The area where I was standing had row after row of golf carts. These carts were different from the carts I used back here in the States. These carts held two bags of clubs and no seats. As I continued to stand videoing the course I heard a Japanese golfer speak loudly. I turned and saw a golf cart moving toward me unattended. It was moving on its own power. I stepped aside and watched the cart pass me. Following the moving cart were two Japanese golfers. As they passed me they bowed and spoke a Japanese greeting. The cart moved a few more feet and stopped. The two golfers took their golf bags from the cart and headed into the clubhouse.

At the same time my friend came out of the club house and walked up to me. I asked him about the moving carts. He gave me a small black box similar to a small transistor radio. It had a red button in the center of the box. He told me to attach the box to my belt and press the button. As I followed his instruction he pointed to an area where several carts were parked and one began to move on its own power. He told me that was our cart. The course was small compared to the golf courses here in the States. This particular course was constructed on descending sections. You began on the highest level and each green was built on a lower level. So as you continued to play each tee was at a lower level than the previous tee. Half way between the tee and the green was a sign that read: The cart automatically stops here. I asked my friend what if I wasn't near this area. He told me that I could stop and make the car proceed by simply pressing the button. I also found out that if you tried to let your golf cart continue toward the golf cart in front of you without pressing the button to stop the cart before hitting the other cart that your cart automatically would stop on its own. It had a built-in cutoff switch.

We had descended down to the eighth green. As I prepared to putt my ball into the cup, I looked around and saw that the 9th hole was way up on top of all these hills. My friend told me to press the button. The cart began to climb the hill and a tram came down on the other side of the invisible cart track. We walked over to the tram, opened the door, touched the go switch and traveled up the hill to the 9th tee. When we reached the top of the hill our cart was stopped at the tee box for the 9th hole. What an experience that was for me.

Originally I had planned to visit these cities in Japan by using the bullet train. However, just before I left the States for Japan the earthquake hit Kobe and many of the railroad tracks were destroyed. I thought that I wouldn't have the opportunity to take a ride on one of those fast trains. I was mistaken. After playing golf Takuji and Mr. Yamamoto took me to the train station. Trains out of Toyohashi were not affected by the earthquake but some of the areas that I would be visiting had no rail service because of the damage to the tracks.

As I stood on the platform at the station Takuji told me to look to my left way up the track. The white dot I saw was the bullet train. There were two sets of tracks passing through the station. The track farthest away from the platform was for the bullet train and the track nearest the platform was the local train. I got my camera ready to photograph the speeding bullet train but I was too slow. In the next second it flew by me at a great speed and continued rapidly down the track. In a few minutes the local pulled into the station, we made our way into the train and found some seats. The train was stopped for only a few minutes when the doors closed and the train began to move. I was seated in the first row of the car next to Mr. Yamamoto. On the wall in front of me was a shelf. A porter approached us and Mr. Yamamoto purchased two cups of coffee, one for me and the other for himself. I set my cup on the shelf in front of me. I watched to see if the coffee would spill but it stood almost still with only a little vibration. The train was moving but the ride was extremely smooth. I gazed out of the window and was amazed at how fast we were moving. Telephone poles and houses seemed to zip past us quickly. I learned later that the local trains travel at a speed of 145 miles an hour.

We exited the train at the next stop and began walking down the street. It was graduation time at this city's local high school. The young girls were dressed in beautiful colorful kimonos. I tried to take a picture of a group of girls but the street was so crowded with people that I couldn't get a picture. Mr. Yamamoto spoke to the group of girls and told them I wanted to photograph them. They moved to the side of the street and posed for a picture.

We continued to walk, looking at the shops and the crowd of people passing by. Mr. Yamamoto went into one of the shops and came out with a beautiful parasol. Takuji said he wanted to buy a gift for Elaine. I thanked him for his thoughtfulness and said Elaine would really enjoy his gift.

We walked back to the train station and took the local back to Toyohashi. The next day I said goodbye to the Yamazaki's and my new found Japanese friend, Mr. Yamamoto. This was a little emotional for both Mr. Yamamoto and me because despite the language barrier we enjoyed each other's company.

## Iwakuni

Takuji drove me to Iwakuni. I joined Wayne & Melody Halla and their two daughters. Wayne was the pastor of an English-speaking Bible church in Iwakuni. A large U.S. Marine Air Corps Station was located at Iwakuni. Most of the church members were marines. Wayne arrange for me to tour the base and be escorted by two of the pilots that attended the Bible church. I had to slip on protective booties because the jet planes were fully equipped and ready for battle. They were sprayed with a special coating to prevent the enemy from detecting the plane on their radar. By wearing these booties you would not scuff up the fuselage of the air craft. Any scuff marks would allow the enemy to pick up the plane on their radar system. I was allowed to climb up onto the wing and look into the cockpit. However, I was not permitted to take any pictures of the interior of the cockpit.

The first night with the Hallas was exciting even though I slept soundly through it. At breakfast I was asked if I felt the earthquake during the night. I said that I hadn't but it didn't matter because I had to sleep on the floor and thus would not have rolled out of bed during the quake.

I spoke at the morning worship service the next day. It was an unusual service because they did not have a person to play the piano or the organ. Instead they had a computerized program that when you called out the number of the hymn to be sung in the hymn book, the computer produced the piano background.

214

# Hiroshima

The following day the Halla family drove me to see the Peace Park at Hiroshima. I walked through the museum built to show the effects of the atomic bomb. They made a model of the atomic bomb that was dropped on August 6, 1945 called the "Little Boy." Alongside the model of the bomb "Little Boy" was a model of the B-29 bomber, the "Enola Gay," that had dropped the bomb on their city. In another part of the museum were wax figurines to show the effects of the bomb on the people. They had men, women and children walking with their skins peeling off their bodies making a very gruesome image of what took place on that historic day.

In the center of the park they erected a monument with an eternal flame. They also left standing a large building that showed the effects of the damage the bomb had done. All of this was a reminder of what took place on that dreadful day.

The day was spent doing some sightseeing around Iwakuni. That evening several airmen and their wives along with Wayne and Melody took me to a Japanese restaurant. It would be my last night to be with the marines and the Halla family.

# Kawachi

The next day Wayne took me to the airport in Iwakuni. I was to fly to the Mahar's in Kawachi. Since no trains were running there because of the earthquake damage, those needing to travel had to use the small commuter planes. Since I could not speak Japanese, Wayne purchased my ticket for me. He said goodbye and I made my way to the gate to board the plane. As I stood in line with mostly Japanese businessmen, I began to realize that here I was in a country where the language was totally unknown to me. However, I had perfect peace and was not at all intimidated by the circumstances. I found my seat on the plane and during the flight found out that the man seated next to me although

Japanese could speak English very well. He was able to assist me when the plane landed.

I spent the next two days with Jon and Mitsy Mahar. Jon had developed Bible lessons in Japanese and would also teach English at a night school there in Kawachi.

Jon took me to the airport and, as did Wayne, he purchased the ticket for me. Once again I found myself in line, the only American in the bunch. The procedure was the same as before on my flight from Iwakuni to Kawachi. I found my seat quite easily. During the flight as before, the man beside me, though Japanese, could speak English. We landed safely at Iwakuni. Wayne was there to take me back to their home and I would prepare to leave for home the next day.

After breakfast Wayne took me back again to the airport in Iwakuni. He purchased the ticket for me and I said my final goodbyes. I made my way to the counter to check in my one suitcase. I was the first in line and by now really ready to go home. There were two clerks to service the long line of passengers. I would take this small commuter plane to Osaka where I would take a plane directly to the U.S. The two clerks were looking at me and speaking rather rapidly in Japanese. I had no idea what they were saying to me and since I was first in line I was determined not to move and lose my spot. I turned around hoping someone behind me would serve as my interpreter. No one volunteered but I sensed the men behind me were getting restless. One of the clerks held up a sign written in English that said "Your luggage is overweight you will be charged extra." Now the one suitcase that I was checking in was the same suitcase that several days before had passed through this same airport without question. The only change was that I had more dirty wash on the dirty wash side than on the previous trip. I replied, pointing to my chest and extending my arm straight out I said; "Me no pay eh, me no pay eh." The clerk responded with some more Japanese words and then said: "OK." I took my ticket and boarded the small commuter plane and flew to Osaka for my long flight home.

[I interrupt my story because as I am writing this it is June 4th, 2016, a very special day in our lives. It is our 61st wedding anniversary. We haven't planned anything special but decided to take the day as it comes. Elaine has been busy doing laundry and cleaning the house. I have elected to continue writing my life story. Roxann and Jim sent us Edible Fruit covered with a chocolate coating. Rick and Tracy sent us a hummingbird feeder and a cute little birdhouse. They made our day.]

Now back to my story. I landed at Osaka international airport to a mass of travelers all making their way to their individual terminals. I stood momentarily trying to get my bearings and where I needed to go. I hadn't been standing looking around for very long when I was approached by an American businessman. He asked me if I was flying back to the States. I told him I was but was just trying to find my way to my terminal. He asked me what flight I would be flying home on and when I responded, he said that it was the same flight he was using. He asked me to follow him to the terminal and he would assist me in any way. He was flying first class but I would be seated in economy class.

After checking in my luggage I began walking down a long corridor to the area where I would board the plane. Half-way down the corridor I noticed a U.S. Marine putting money into a large machine that resembled a cigarette machine. I saw him insert some money and receive a piece of paper in return. I inquired as to what he was doing and he told me that you needed this pass in order to take the tram to be able to board the plane. All I had was a few American dollars and as I looked at my watch I knew that I didn't have enough time to make a money exchange. Just then I remembered the honorarium that I had received the first Sunday I preached in Toyohashi. I was wearing the same sport coat that I had worn when I preached that Sunday and remembered that I had put the Japanese money in my pocket. To my utter surprise the honorarium was the exact amount needed to purchase the pass for the tram. Once again I acknowledged God's plan for my life and what I was doing was what He called me to do.

Soon we were seated in the plane and a short time later we left Osaka, Japan heading toward J. F. Kennedy Airport in New York City. I counted it a great privilege to have been able to visit our missionaries in Japan and see so many sights in so many cities.

# Mexico

## *Guadalajara*

I arrived in Guadalajara on a bright, hot, sunny day. Mark and Carole Landis have been missionaries in this large city for many years. Mark met me at the airport and took me to their home. He told me that a short time before I arrived there was an accident at one of the large gas stations. For some reason a large amount of gasoline had leaked into the sewer system resulting in a huge explosion. He would take me the next day to see the damage. After breakfast Mark and Carole drove me to where we could see the extent of the damage. There was a six-foot ravine down the middle of the street that had to be blocked off from any traffic. I walked over to a spot that was shallow enough to step down and make my way to the bottom of the ravine. Mark took my picture standing in the middle of the ravine. As I looked around at the extent of the damage I saw the remains of a large apartment building with several walls still standing. Also seen were the remains of a bathroom. Part of the bathroom floor and back wall was still intact supporting the bathtub.

While driving into the heart of the city we had to drive defensively. Cars were speeding all around us but the real hazard was the open areas in the street where manhole covers once covered the hole. The blast had hurled them from their resting place to other parts of the roadbed. There were no markers to identify the open holes so the drivers had to swerve at the last minute to avoid driving into them.

We stopped to look at one of the city's largest Catholic cathedrals. I watched as Catholics young and old were crawling up the many steps into the church. This is their way to show humility before entering the church to pray and worship.

218

Over the years of service in Guadalajara, the Landis's had established a Bible Institute and several churches. I would be speaking through an interpreter to the entire student body on several occasions. I also had the privilege to visit several churches that were pastored by students of the Bible Institute on the following Sunday. I remember very plainly eating breakfast before visiting the churches and what took place at that time. I usually wore a dress shirt and a tie. I was dressed as I sat down to eat my breakfast. Carole gave me a peeled mango and as I began eating it, it slipped out of my hand and landed on my tie. I am glad that Elaine had packed several ties for me so changing to another was no problem.

I spent the week with Mark, Carole and the students of La Roca Bible Institute. Most of the student body was together in a group singing a song for me and saying goodbye in Spanish as Mark and Carole drove me to the airport for my trip back home.

# England & Scotland

## *Blackburn & London*

In the early days of FIM when it was called Moroccan Evangelical Mission and Mary Mellinger and Irene Whenholtz had begun the orphanage in Azrou Morocco, Miss Rokeby Robinson, a single lady from England who had set up a clinic in Itzer some 50 miles from Azrou and did mainly midwife assistance, would come to the Haven when Mary and Irene needed help. The Haven nicknamed her "Robin." She would visit the Haven from time to time and assist in any way possible. She served in her clinic and at the Haven for many years before retiring and moving to London.

One of the couples from First Baptist Church in Phillipsburg was an architect and did work with a mission agency that specialized in building buildings for missionary needs. Bruce and Jerry Watson worked with Helps International Ministries and had been transferred from North Carolina to Blackburn, England to open a new office for the mission. They were eager to learn that I wanted to come to London and visit the retired veteran missionary. They wanted me to come to visit them, then Bruce would accompany me to London to visit the elderly missionary.

Bruce and Jerry met me at the airport. What a happy reunion because we had not seen each other for a considerable amount of time. Their home was small and cozy. I enjoyed talking with them and their children as they remembered their days at First Baptist.

Bruce and Jerry attended a small Plymouth Brethren Church in Blackburn. The morning service was open only to members of the church. Bruce and Jerry had not joined at that time so we did not go to church in the morning. Sunday school was offered in the afternoon and open to everyone. Before I arrived Bruce had spoken to the elders of the church and informed them that I would be visiting with them. The elders invited me to speak at the evening preaching service which was also open to everyone whether members or not. I was welcomed warmly and the people were very friendly. After the evening service the Watsons had invited several people to join with us at their home for some snacks and fellowship.

The next day Bruce, Jerry, their children and I drove into the English countryside. We stopped at an old church that had been badly burned. The story of the burning includes a King that wanted to divorce his wife and marry another woman but the Bishop declined to perform the ceremony. The King in turn set the church on fire. All that remained were the high stone walls. Sometime later a small chapel was built using the back wall as the starting point of the building. We walked around the burnt structure and made our way to the back of the old church. The parking lot was filled with cars and we could hear beautiful music. As we came closer to the entrance of the chapel we saw that we were witnessing a wedding. We only stayed awhile in the foyer of the chapel listening to the music sung by the choir.

We left the chapel and continued to drive through the countryside until we approached a large castle. Blackburn, England was only a short distance from Scotland and we had crossed over into Scotland. It was interesting to tour around the old castle.

We left the castle and drove a short distance to a small town with cobblestone streets. It was a very quaint Scottish town with shops and houses lining the streets. On the corner of one of the streets we stopped for lunch at a pub. The inside was small and compact with exposed old wooden beams, dark wood tables and chairs. We ordered lunch and I had one of the best shepherd's pie I had ever eaten.

The next day Bruce and I made our way to London to visit Miss Rokeby Robinson who had assisted Mary Mellinger and Irene Whenholtz for so many years at the Children's Haven in Morocco. We boarded the train at Blackburn and traveled several hours to London. After walking for several blocks, we were able to locate the small apartment for which we were looking. We knocked on the door and were welcomed by a smiling elderly lady. She invited us in and asked us to have a seat. She went to her little kitchen and began to make us all some tea. It was a very enjoyable visit learning more about the history of the Children's Haven and of her life's story. Soon it was time for us to leave her and begin our return trip to Blackburn.

We walked back toward the railroad station and in a very busy area of London we stopped for a bite to eat. We had an enjoyable meal and reached the station in time to catch the train back to Blackburn. It was late that night when we reached home – exhausted but happy for the enjoyable day. Before we all retired for the night I thanked Bruce and Jerry for the opportunity to visit with them and for their taking the time to show me many sights. I wanted to make sure I said goodbye to the children because early the next morning I needed to leave for Paris, France.

Very early the next morning Bruce took me to the airport and I boarded a plane for Paris.

# France

## *Paris*

Trevor Kocote, one of our FIM Canadian missionaries, was assisting several other missionaries in establishing a church in Paris. He was to meet me at Charles de Gaulle International airport. I claimed my luggage and waited for quite a long time looking for Trevor to appear. It was about an hour later and still no Trevor, so I made my way to the center of this vast airport and asked the attendant if she would be kind enough to have Trevor paged. She replied that she was sorry but that was against airport policy. I had no other choice but to just stay where I was and hope Trevor would soon be here.

Sometime later he arrived. I am not sure how long it was but to me it had taken forever for him to arrive. He apologized because he thought he told me to go to Orly International Airport on the other side of Paris. When he rechecked our correspondence, he saw he had made the mistake. He came to Charles de Gaulle as fast as he could.

Now the fun began. Trevor did not have a car and used public transportation to travel around the city. He was able to borrow a car from a friend and drive to the airport to pick me up. We walked for a long time trying to find the car. Not only did we have a hard time locating the car but the ride back to Trevor's apartment was a real nightmare. The French people drive crazy. This, added to the fact that Trevor hadn't driven a car for some time, made my car trip with him a real challenge.

Before returning the car Trevor took me on a short trip around Paris. We drove though the Arc de Triomphe and stopped at the Eiffel Tower. We didn't take the opportunity to do more than walk around the area and pass by the many sidewalk cafes. Trevor needed to get back to his friends who were busy remodeling a rented room they were using as their church. It was late in the afternoon when we arrived. I was introduced to the small group of mostly young people who welcomed me warmly. The group had brought in some food because they had planned to work on the remodeling, have something to eat and hold a service before going to their homes. I noticed a bakery several doors from their church and had Trevor accompany me so that I could buy some baked goods for the meal. It was hard to make a selection because everything looked so good that I wanted to take a taste of it.

After the evening service Trevor took me back to his apartment. The next morning we toured the Louvre Museum and, one of the large railroad stations, Gare du Nord, the Eiffel Tower and other tourist attractions. I had talked with him about the possibility of driving me to Brussels to visit with Donna Hegge, another FIM Canadian missionary. If he could get the use of his friend's car I would pay for the gasoline to make the trip.

Early the next morning we began our trip driving through parts of France that had been the battlefield of World War II. It was 109-mile trip one way and looking at the scenery along the way was fascinating.

# Belgium

## *Brussels*

Donna was waiting for us when we arrived. We went to her apartment and listened to her describe her musical ministry there in Brussels. Later she took us on a tour of Brussels showing us the park where the World's Fair was held from April to October in 1958. We stopped at a local restaurant for something to eat before starting back to Paris. The interior was similar to the pub in Scotland with its ornate wooden beams and aged wood seating. While we were enjoying our meal, the door to the restaurant was open and a stray dog trotted in making his way among the tables. Donna told us that wasn't a problem at all because that was the way of life here.

We thanked Donna for her hospitality and began our return trip to Paris. It soon became dark and the moon was bright and clear. We continued to drive well into the night when I asked Trevor if he knew the way back to Paris. He said he was simply following the moon. I knew he was serious because we had been driving for a considerable amount of time and had not reached our destination. I became concerned because we had been on the road for several hours and the next morning I needed to be on a plane to Sweden for our annual advisory meeting.

It was very late when we actually arrived at Trevor's apartment. I didn't waste any time getting my things ready for the trip to Sweden the next morning. I reminded Trevor that we would have to leave for the airport at 4:00 am. By now I had seen enough of Trevor to know his makeup was a "comme ci comme ca" attitude. I am so glad I set my alarm clock because I had to go to Trevor's room and get him awake. He had forgotten to set his alarm clock before he went to sleep.

We made a hasty trip to the airport and I caught my plane to Stockholm. I made this trip several years in a row but this trip would be my last to serve on the Advisory Board. My stay this time in Sweden was short and I soon would fly back to the States.

# Ecuador

### *Quito*

Bill Ridgeway met me at the Quito airport. As we walked out of the airport Bill told me to take my time as we walked because I was now almost 10,000 feet above sea level and the air is thin. Being a Pennsylvania Dutchman it had to be proven to me to be true. So I started to walk as if I was back home and almost immediately I felt some pressure on my chest. Breathing in that thin air certainly is a different reaction on your lungs than walking back home. I stayed with Bill and Irene for a short time before Bill took me to meet Morley Johnson.

Morley and Darlene Johnson worked mainly with the Quechua Indians in the Chimborazo section of the Andes Mountains. Morley had been working with the Quechuas for several years. He was instrumental in developing a safe drinking water system and was now working on a sanitation system.

I accompanied Morley on a trip to a Quechua council meeting of the church leaders at a Quechua village high in the Chimborazo Mountain range. Morley had a small Toyota pickup truck that he used to haul materials and also served as his personal mode of transportation.

We began our trip up the mountain early on a Sunday morning. The road was a one lane gravel road. Morley explained that this road was used for traffic both ways and that as we went up the mountain you would see turn offs on the left side of the road for vehicles coming down the mountain to pull into so that the vehicle coming up the mountain could pass safely. There were no turn offs traveling up the mountain and no guard rails to protect a vehicle from going over the edge of the mountain road on the right side of the road. There were accidents of vehicles traveling up the mountain road, losing control and driving off the road falling over the edge to their deaths. No one was able to try to search for the vehicle or the passengers because of the sheer drop of over 10,000 ft. The only thing that was done was to place a cross at the point where the vehicle went off the side of the road and tumbled down the mountain.

We had gone about half way up the mountain when a large Ford pickup truck was coming down the mountain. That individual did not pull into a turn off area and we found ourselves trying to squeeze past as the truck came along side us. I looked over at the driver of the Ford and it seemed that he didn't even see us. Morley said that the driver was probably drunk. At that moment I was glad we were in a small Toyota truck because if we were in a bigger vehicle we would have been forced off the road and over the edge to our deaths.

We finally arrived at our destination. We were welcomed by the Quechua leaders and invited to join them for the council meeting. Several minutes into the meeting an old Quechua Indian came into the room and gave Morley and me a bottle of Coca Cola. He hadn't been gone long when another Quechua came into the room and presented us with a sleeve of Ritz crackers. A short time later a third Quechua entered the room and presented us with a vacuum sealed block of cheese. This may seem as an everyday occurrence to us here in the States, but you need to remember that these Quechua's are very poor and the next town that had a store was many miles away.

Morley had notified the leaders that we would be coming to join them at their council meeting. Word had spread through their village and they made plans to greet us with these gifts. Jobs were scarce and their wages very meager. They must have pooled their money together in order to be able to purchase these things for us. It was a very moving experience for me to witness their desire to honor us with these gifts.

The meeting was over and we were escorted around the village. Their huts were mostly made of mud and manure. I had to duck down low in order to enter through the door. Their average height is about 4 to 4 1/2 ft.

As I walked around the village I took notice that there were several cinder block homes among the huts. Morley explained to me the difference between the two homes. The Quechua women did most of the work in providing for their family. I saw women taking their children, a donkey and some gardening tools, and walking to another part of the village to work in their gardens. The men usually sat around drinking and doing very little work to benefit their families. However, when a Quechua man accepted Christ he began to change his habits. He found work, began saving his money and when he had saved enough, he built a new house with cinder block and tore down the old mud and manure hut. So everywhere I saw a cinder block home it was a home of a believer. To me this was a very vivid picture of the meaning behind II Corinthians 5:17: "Therefore if any man be in Christ, he is a new creature; old things are passed away; behold all things are become new."

Next Morley took me to see the latest improvement that he had brought to this village. He had arranged to bring a large loom up the mountain. He rewired the loom so that the low voltage electricity they had in the village would be sufficient to run the loom. Now the Quechuas could use the loom to weave blankets and clothing, and other items. It was a way for the Indians to sell their merchandise and have a way to make a living.

After spending the day with the Quechuas we drove back down the mountain to the town of Riobamba. Morley had arranged for us to spend the night at the local hotel. This was quite an experience. My room was small but adequate. The bed was nothing more than some boards with a thin mattress. The bathroom was small as well but again adequate. Tight against the base of the hopper was a small wall about four inches high to keep the water into the shower area. This meant that if you sat on the toilet your right leg would have to extend over the shower wall.

I was covered with dust from traveling down the mountain on the dirt roads. I prepared to take a shower but I discovered that no matter which water valve I turned on I would only get cold water. Try as I may no matter how long I left the water run it still was cold. I later found out that the hotel only supplied lukewarm water very early in the morning. Since my hair was covered with dust I decided to turn on the shower and just quickly stick my head in so that at least the dust would be washed out. I set my alarm clock to go off at 3:00 am so that I could take advantage of a warm water shower.

I just started to fall asleep when there was quite a racket in the next room. I got out of bed and went next door. I knocked on the door and was greeted by several men. Since I didn't know much Spanish, I put my finger to my mouth as a sign of silence then with my two hands clasped together I rested them on my head at an angle as a sign that I was sleeping. The men nodded and shut the door. The noise ceased and I fell back to sleep.

When the alarm went off I turned on the hot water in the shower. It was lukewarm but good enough to get a quick shower. Before I went back to be with the Ridgeways, Morley took me to the Missionary

Aviation Fellowship base where the five missionaries flew into the jungle to make contact with the Auca Indians. All five were eventually murdered by them. I was offered a ride by plane to those Indians who were now no longer savages, but I had to decline because of the time schedule that was earlier established.

Morley drove me to the place where I would meet up again with the Ridgeways. I would be with Bill and Irene for a short time before leaving from Quito airport to return home. On the way back to the Ridgeway's home Bill took me to see HCJB radio headquarters in Quito. It is quite an operation with a wide range of broadcasting Christian radio.

We next stopped at San Antonio. In this town is a park called the Metad del Mundo (the middle of the earth). There is a 98 ½ ft. stone pyramid with a 15 ft. globe on the top. This pyramid is built on the equator and there is a marked line down through the park designating where the equator is located. You can straddle the equator by putting one foot on one side of the equator and your right foot on the other side of the equator. I walked up the steps on the inside of the pyramid to the observation level. From there you can see the entire park and town below.

We took one last stop with the Ridgeways before going back to their home. They took me to a woodworking shop near to Meta del Mundo Park where the owner made a rocker out of a special kind of wood. The back and seat was made of thick leather. The back piece of leather has the picture of the pyramid and the Chimborazo Mountains etched into the leather. The seat has an etched picture of a Quechua Indian man and woman with some scenery. The chair is designed to be easily taken apart and quickly put back together again. The legs and arm pieces of wood are marked with numbers and the leather seat and back are held in place with wooden pegs. I just had to have that chair. The cost was over $100.00 and that was more than I had in my wallet. The only way for me to purchase the chair and bring it home with me was to charge it on my credit card. And charge it I did. The chair after being disassembled fit nicely into a box about 32 inches high by 4 inches wide. To this day that chair is in my office and is quite a conversation piece.

Bill loaded the chair into the car and we were on our way back to the Ridgeway's. After the evening meal I packed my suitcase and got ready for my return trip home the next day.

Shortly after we had eaten, Bill received word that a city-wide riot was to take place the next day. When they had these riots the rioters would pile car and truck tires in the streets to set them on fire. They would block every main road in and out of the city. To avoid this problem, we left very early in the morning in order to get to the airport before the riots began. This we successfully accomplished and I was able to get to the airport and board my plane to come home.

As I began my travels to visit personally with those missionaries serving in those countries I discovered that on the foreign field the word "Independent" in our mission's name didn't mean what it had originally meant when instituted. Some of the missionaries were not even using our name. I realized that we needed to change the name to emphasize who we were as a missionary sending agency. I presented the problem to the Board of Directors and made the suggestion that we remove the word "Independent" and replace it with the word "International." The board unanimously approved and our new name now was: "Fellowship International Mission."

We are a "Fellowship," a family of individuals serving the Lord. We are "International" because we have missionaries serving around the world. Lastly, we are a bona fide "Mission," properly and legally established and recognized by the U.S. Government.

Sao Paulo, Brazil

Francisco & Elaine de Souza and staff, Capinas, Brazil

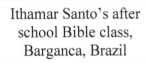

Ithamar Santo's after school Bible class, Barganca, Brazil

Stockholm, Sweden

230

John & Judy Breneman and family, Garbo, Sweden

Doug & Judy Jackson and family, Uppsala, Sweden

Me with Rea Andes, Warragul, Australia

Feeding a kangaroo

Arthur & Dorothy and David
Johns, Brisbane, Australia

Marilyn Hutchinson & Linda
Hochman, Sydney, Australia

Grace Baptist Church,
Toyohashi, Japan

Preaching at Grace Baptist
Church

| Pastor Yamasaki and family, Toyohashi, Japan | Authentic Japanese meal |

| Mr. Yamamoto, my friend | Playing golf in Japan |

Ride on local
bullet train

Railroad station,
Toyohashi, Japan

Hiroshima
Peace Park

Wayne & Melody Halla and
family, Iwakuni, Japan

Jon & Mitsy Mahar and family, Ishikawa, Japan

Watson family at castle in Harwich, Scotland

Cobblestone street, Harwich, Scotland

Me with Trevor Kocote, Paris, France

Eiffel Tower,
Paris, France

Donna Hegge,
Brussels, Belguim

Bill & Irene Ridgeway,
Quito, Ecuador

Me with two Quecha
Indian Pastors, near
Riobamba, Ecuador

Morley Johnson with Quecha Indian leaders, Ecuador

Bill Ridgeway, Meta de Mundo, Ecuador

Missionary Aviation base, Ecuador

15 ft. globe on top of monument, Meta de Mundo, Ecuador

237

# Retirement

After serving for ten years, I reached the point in my life that I knew it was time for me to step aside and let a younger man take the reins. I felt I had gone as far as I could in bringing the mission to this point and now new leadership would be able to continue the outreach and purpose for which FIM was begun.

I met with the President of the Board of Directors and informed him of my decision to step down from leadership. I submitted my resignation to become effective January 1, 2000.

In April of 2000 we moved from Forks Township in Easton, PA to the Fairways at Brookside, Macungie, PA. We found a wonderful condo with all the rooms on one floor. It is a quiet community with friendly neighbors. On several occasions we would entertain several couples with whom we had fellowship from First Baptist Church and the Fellowship Church. They expressed how wonderful our condo was laid out inside and with spacious lawns outside. One of the couples was Bob and Betty Lutz who were presently living in Riegelsville, NJ. This was something that they thought they might be interested in sometime in the future. Betty was interested in living here but Bob was reluctant because he enjoyed working around their home especially in the spring and summer months doing the entire yard work.

It wasn't but several months later that Bob was mowing the lawn at their home in Riegelsville, NJ when he accidently ran the mower into a wasp nest. He was bitten on several areas of his body. In a short time, he began to swell up and Betty rushed him to Warren Hospital in Phillipsburg, NJ. This was a traumatic experience for them both. After receiving medical attention Bob and Betty returned to their home in Riegelsville. They began discussing what they should do since this was the first time that it had happened to him. They were concerned about all the yard work that they enjoyed doing. There was the lawn to mow, the bushes and shrubs to trim and, in the fall, the raking of the leaves. They both enjoyed their home since they had had it built shortly after they were married so many years ago. It was the place they raised their family and entertained guests. It would be a hard decision to sell the house but the experience that occurred with the wasp stings was powerful enough to have them thinking about the next move.

It was about this same time that we noticed that our neighbors in the unit behind us had not returned from their Florida winter home. They would usually stay in Florida for six months and live here for the other six months. I decided to ask the Fairways manager about our neighbors. I was told that they were going to remain in Florida and put their condo up for sale. I explained to him our interest in the unit and he graciously gave me the phone number of the unit owner in Florida. I passed this information on to Bob and Betty and they in turn made the phone call. Before long we received a phone call from two excited people. Bob and Betty had purchased the condo behind us and would begin making arrangements to move here. There was a lot to do in getting their house sold, but it didn't take long for them to find a buyer and complete the transaction. The moving date was set and in a short time we had new neighbors.

This began a very enjoyable relationship. We played games, ate at each other's homes, took trips to shopping malls and for our birthdays we drove to Lancaster to drive through the countryside and see the sights. At the end of the day our last stop was Shady Maple buffet. The person celebrating their birthday was treated to a free all-you-can-eat meal. Many times after getting things done around the house in the morning and seeing that it was a beautiful day outside, we called Bob and Betty on the spur of the moment and invited them to go with us to do errands or take a ride somewhere.

Bob loved to fish and every summer he and Paul Robison would drive to the Jersey shore, rent a boat and spend the day fishing in the bay. This was a custom they had begun many years before and they enjoyed the day with or without any fish.

Bob and I began talking about fishing here for trout. All four of us purchased lifetime fishing licenses with the trout stamp affixed. We all tried our hand at fishing a few times but the girls found that it really didn't appeal to them so it was just Bob and me. We joined a fishing club a few miles from our home and fished for several years together. Sometimes we brought fish home and other times we just enjoyed the day by the water.

It was on one warm spring night as we were enjoying our snack on our patio that we began talking about planning a trip somewhere for a few days. Elaine and I had been to Nova Scotia over ten years previous when we joined with Ed and Mary Jane Savacool for the trip. We shared some of our experiences with Bob and Betty Lutz and they thought it would be the kind of trip they would appreciate.

Our trip with the Savacools had been taken in October. We drove to Maine on our first day, found a quaint restaurant for our evening meal and checked into a motel. The next day we crossed into Canada and stopped at New Brunswick to visit Hopewell Rocks on the Bay of Fundy. We parked on the parking lot at the Bay of Fundy visitor center. On a nearby building we could see the picture of the bay and several rules and regulations. We read that the tide rises to a height of 56 feet quite rapidly there and those who would choose to walk on the beach should be aware of this danger.

At the end of the walk way we could look over the edge down to the beach. The tide was out so we decided to climb down the ladder placed over the edge of the cliff leading to the beach. One by one we all climbed down the ladder and soon we were taking a stroll on the beach. We hadn't wandered far from the ladder when we noticed that the water had begun to rise. The tide was coming in. In a flash we remembered the warning we had read on the park's bulletin board. No one said anything, but instinctively we all headed back to the ladder as fast as we could.

One by one we climbed the ladder as fast as possible. Back on the ledge of the cliff we could see the water rapidly climbing up the ladder we had just exited. That was one of our exhilarating experiences on this trip because the tide at this point rises to over 40 feet in a very short time.

The next several days we toured some of the major cities of Nova Scotia. Since it was past the major tourist season, some of the places of interest were closed especially many restaurants. We did however find several quaint places to eat that we really enjoyed. Ed had a baked sausage and sauerkraut dinner at a small German restaurant that he talked about the whole trip.

On Halloween night we stayed at a bread and breakfast in a small town. When we registered we were told that this old building was haunted and especially on Halloween night. We ate our evening meal at a small restaurant near the B&B. After we ate we went back to the B&B and relaxed in the quaint and comfortable living room. The fireplace was warm and the flame burned in a uniform manner and not what we would see in our fireplace. I learned that they were burning coke and the flame was more uniform and consistent. I wanted to take a picture so I went back to our room to get my camera. When we left our room after preparing to go for supper, Elaine pulled down all the shades in our room. I remember what we were told about the place being haunted on Halloween night and I deliberately pulled all the shades up. I came back to the living room and took some pictures.

While we were sitting and talking we heard a band playing outside. We all went to the big bay window and watched a marching band of about a dozen individuals playing their instruments and marching down the street. We saw little children carrying pillow cases to be used as a bag to collect trick or treats. After the band passed by we decided it was time to retire for the night so we could get an early start in the morning. When we opened the door to our room Elaine looked at the windows with all the shades in the up position and said this place is really haunted because I deliberately pulled all the shades down when we went to eat. I had to confess that I was the one who pulled the shades up when I came back to the room for my camera.

We got an early start because we wanted to drive the Cabot trail that circled Cape Breton. It was a chilly October morning and I had to scrape off the frost from the windshield. The sun was shining brightly and as we drove we saw many wonderful sights. I stopped at several places to take some pictures. It was about mid-afternoon when we began the long descent down the other side of the island. We were driving into the sun's rays and could feel its warmth in the car. To my amazement everyone was fast asleep, leaving the driving to me. As I drove I could see a large area of the beach very close to the road. I slowed down and parked the car. Now everyone was wide awake. We decided to take a walk along the beach and watch the waves rush onto the shore. Elaine and I had started a practice that we would collect small stones from where we had traveled and bring them home with us. We would place them into small jars as a reminder of those trips. So we began collecting different stones that had washed up onto the beach. We had collected quite a few stones of various colors when we noticed a very pretty greenish stone lying a few feet in the water. As we reached down to pick up the stone a huge wave came rushing in and before we could move out of the way it hit Elaine with such force that she was knocked down into the cold sea water. It was hard to hold back the laughter. Not only was her clothing soaked but her hair as well. Now you need to know that Elaine would go in our pool to float around but would never put her head under water. So this was quite an unusual situation. I helped her up and walked her back to the car shivering as she walked. Ed and Mary Jane continued on their walk on the beach. Elaine had to go into the suitcase in the trunk of the car, get out fresh clothes, and climb in the back seat and re-dress. Once she was dressed we all got back into the car and continued on our trip. This, of course, was quite a conversation piece for the rest of our stay in Nova Scotia. We all agreed that we had a wonderful time in Nova Scotia.

After hearing of our adventures with Ed and Mary Jane, Bob and Betty were enthusiastic about planning a trip to Nova Scotia. We talked more about the trip and thought it would be great to go for about ten days including a stopover at Prince Edward Island. That suited all of us and it was agreed that I should map out the trip to show them what areas we should plan to visit.

At our next meeting together discussing the route we would be taking, we decided that I should drive but whose car should we use. Rather than take either car we agreed that we would rent a car but needed to see what the costs would be. The next day Bob and I went to Enterprise Car Rental and discussed our plans with the agent. We wanted a car with a large enough trunk for all the suitcases and necessities that we said the ladies always needed to take along just in case. After looking at what was available we were given the costs on a Cadillac. At first the figures he quoted appeared that we would be buying the car. I began to negotiate and finally arrived at a feasible figure. The papers were signed and the dates set. We would be using the car for a total of ten days with no mileage charges.

About a week before we were to pick up the car I went back to the Enterprise office to recheck on our arrangements. The attendant said he wasn't sure he could get the car. I reminded him of our signed rental agreement and told him I expected to pick up the car on the designated day.

The big day finally arrived. The suitcases were packed, snacks packed and everything else the ladies thought they needed. The only thing left for Bob and I to do was to pick up the car at Enterprise. We walked through the office door and were greeted by the gentlemen that had written up the rental agreement. He smiled and handed us the keys to a fire engine red, four-door Cadillac sedan with less than a thousand miles on the odometer. We thanked him, took the keys, drove the car back home and began loading the trunk. It was time for supper and then early to bed so we could get an early start the next morning.

Dawn came and we were happily on our way. We hadn't driven very far when Bob exclaimed that his seat was freezing cold and getting colder. We discovered that he accidently hit the seat air-conditioning button on the armrest of his door. That was quickly corrected and we had an uneventful trip, ending the day in Bangor, Maine.

As we started out the second day we had only a few miles to travel until we reached the Canadian border. Sometimes it would take considerable amount of time going through the line and answering all the border guards' questions. As we approached the border we could see that the line was moving quite rapidly. I told Bob that as soon as we were across the border he would be in for a great surprise.
It was only a few minutes and we crossed the border into the town of Saint Stephen, New Brunswick, Canada and there on the corner was Bob's surprise. I pulled up and stopped the car in front of Tim Horton's Coffee shop. I told Bob that he had never tasted a cup of coffee as good as Tim Horton's.

I explained that on my first trip to Calgary, Alberta, Canada to attend FIM Canada's Board of Director's meeting, that Steve Erickson, the President of the Board, had introduced me to my first cup of Tim Horton and I was hooked.

After Bob's first sip he too was hooked. From then on every time we came upon a Tim Horton's coffee shop we had to stop. Getting back into the car we shared some pastries with the ladies, put our coffee cups into the cup holders and drove to view the Bay of Fundy and the rising tide.

Bob and Betty were as excited as we were to see the tide come rushing in. We, however, didn't go down the ladder as we did with Ed and Mary Jane years before.

After watching the tide rise higher and higher, we looked for the last time at the Bay of Fundy and walked back to our car ready for the next stop. We continued driving directly to the bridge that connects Nova Scotia with Prince Edward Island.

We stopped at the entrance to the bridge and paid the toll. On this bridge you pay only one way and your return trip is included in the price. The bridge connects New Brunswick to Prince Edward Island and is the longest bridge ever constructed over ice-covered waters. It is eight miles long and is Canada's greatest engineering project. Our next stop was to check in at Joshua's Outlook B&B. It is a cozy New England style home looking out over the bay. We were greeted by the owners and shown to our rooms. This would be our home away from home for the next three nights.

Our trip around Prince Edward Island would be sightseeing in cities of Charlottetown, Cornwell, Georgetown, Montague and the smaller towns and villages in between. We found great seafood for our lunches and main meals. One of the highlights of our trip to the Island was to tour the House where Lucy Maud Montgomery wrote the "House of Green Gables" in Cavendish.

The next several days we toured the major cities as we mapped out how much of Nova Scotia we could see in the time remaining. We definitely wanted to see the tide come in precisely every twelve hours at the Tidal Bore at Truro and tour the Citadel at Halifax. We would certainly stop enroute at things that would catch our interest. Elaine and Betty could be counted on to do a good job at this.

As we started out for the day making our way to Halifax the sun began to hide behind the clouds. The sun would go in and out of the clouds all day but no rain. Bob and I toured the citadel and the girls walked around the business district of Halifax. We met at our designated location and time. The girls were very excited. They said we had to hurry because they had made reservations to ride the Duck Boat around Halifax and the harbor but they were soon ready to begin the tour. We climbed on board and found four seats on the top deck. We toured around the city looking at the sites and listening to the tour guide explain some of the history of the city. We eventually drove down a narrow street that led to the edge of the water of the bay. It was quite an experience to feel the Duck Boat slide into the water. It was very interesting to look at the many ships docked and look at the city from the water. The Duck Boat found the spot where we would once again be back on land and back to the place where we had begun the tour. After finding a restaurant and enjoying a wonderful meal, we headed for our motel.

After a good night's sleep and a terrific breakfast we were off to Turro to witness the Tidal Bore. We arrived around noon and checked into the Tidal Bore Inn. We had lunch and after talking with the waitress we found out that the tide rises every twelve hours. The next tide is expected at 2:00 pm and then again at 2:00 am. We had enough time to finish our lunch and walk a few hundred yards to see the tide come in. Our motel was located that close to the action.

At 2:00 pm as we stood near the bank of the river, we could hear a slight rushing sound. We watched the water begin to rise higher and higher when suddenly the top of the small wave could be seen approaching where we were standing. The wave covered the entire breadth of the river. As soon as it passed us it was all over. Bob and I determined that we would set our alarm clocks in enough time to come back to watch at 2:00 am. The girls were just as excited to see the Tidal Bore action but not that excited to get out of bed to see it again at 2:00 am.

My alarm went off and I quickly got dressed trying not to disturb Elaine any more than necessary. Bob was waiting outside. It was about twenty-five minutes before the tide would be coming in. It was dark outside but suddenly huge spotlights came on illuminating the entire river in front of us. We were not alone. There was quite a group of people standing there waiting to experience the Tidal Bore. Some of them simply came out in their pajamas and robes to witness this event. As we stood there in silence in the distance we could hear the faint rushing sound. Right on schedule we saw the tide begin to rise and then we saw the wave make it rapidly down the river past us. Bob and I experienced this phenomenon once again. As we made our way back to our rooms, the spotlights were turned off and it was black once again. We learned later that those spotlights are on a timer because the Tidal Bore wave is that precise.

After breakfast we began our trip that would take us back along the shore and eventually to Antigonish. The day began quite dreary and as we drove the rain began to fall quite heavily. I was disappointed because we couldn't see very far out to sea. I wanted Bob and Betty to experience stopping at one of the small fishing villages for a special treat. Usually in these villages one person turned one room of their house into a bake shop. The pastries were out of this world. However because of the rain and fog we had to shelve that idea.

As we drove we all expressed the need to find a restroom. On these roads it was difficult to find a McDonald's or a restaurant until you came into one of the larger towns or cities. We were getting pretty desperate when I saw a sign that read: Krauch J. Willy & Sons Smoked Salmon. The address told us it was at Tanger and the arrow pointed to the left. At the next road I turned left and a short distance we came to a large white structure with a smaller building in the back. It was the place where they smoked the salmon. They also made the front room area into a retail store. We entered to see a large refrigerated showcase with packages of smoked salmon. I also noticed that in the back behind the counter a large sign that read: "Restrooms for employees only." Knowing our desperate need of a restroom I got up enough nerve to sympathetically request that we would be allowed to use the facilities. The owner took pity on us and escorted us upstairs to the restroom.

After we had taken our turns we all went back downstairs and purchased some of the smoked salmon. We posed for a picture with the owner outside of the building under his business sign. The owner gave us his business brochure and said that his company ships his salmon around the world. As we went out the door we thanked him again for his hospitality.

Running between the rain drops we jumped into the car and began to drive back to the main highway to Antigonish. It didn't take the girls long to open the package of smoked salmon and give us a taste. We had a small chest in the back seat between Elaine and Betty with some snacks and bottles of water. The girls passed us some crackers to eat with the salmon. We had never tasted salmon that delicious. I think I only drove a few miles and before we entered the main highway I turned around and went back to buy some more salmon.

It was later that afternoon when we arrived in Antigonish. We checked into the motel and went looking for a restaurant. One thing we all found out on our trip was that we seemed to always find a good place to eat. After a wonderful meal we headed back to the motel. It was still raining heavily. Once inside the motel we decided to play one of the games we had brought along with us. During playing the game we began talking about where to go with the few days we had left. After checking the weather report we learned that we would experience rain for the next few days. That meant that the rest of our time in Nova Scotia would be spent running from the rain drops. I suggested that we leave Nova Scotia in the morning and drive to spend the rest of our vacation in Maine. Everyone was in agreement.

I canceled the arrangements I had made for the nights we would have spent in Nova Scotia. I took the AAA travel booklet that we had with us and found an AAA motel in Ogunquit, Maine. Elaine and I had been to this area of Maine several times with Jim and Roxann. When Jim was scheduled to teach a class at the Eagleson Institute in Sanford, Maine and Roxann could adjust her schedule at the hospital they would invite us to come along with them. The Eagleson family owned a condo in Kennebunkport on the second floor with a balcony facing the ocean. I believe we were fortunate enough to have been there at least six times. On one occasion I had the opportunity to shake hands with President H.W. Bush and his wife, Barbara. So we had lots to show Bob and Betty as we concluded our vacation in Maine.

The last few days of our vacation we enjoyed wonderful weather and had a very enjoyable time but the good days were about to end as we started our return trip back home. One of our last things we did was to drive a few miles from our Motel in Ogunquit to Perkins Cove. Here we walked along the Marginal Way. The Marginal Way is one of New England's only paved public shoreline footpaths. It's about one mile long offering many spectacular views of the Atlantic Ocean shoreline with its many varied rock scenes. After our walk we ate our last meal in Maine because early the next morning we were leaving to drive back home. The trip home went well without any problems. After unpacking Bob and I returned the car to Enterprise and our wonderful relaxing vacation was ended.

After resigning as General Director effective January 1, 2000, I continued to represent FIM in Pastor Fellowship meetings and speaking engagements as General Director Emeritus.

516 Red Fox Lane,
Easton, PA

2724 Rolling Green
Place, Macungie, PA

Bob & Betty Lutz,
condo neighbors and
traveling friends

Great friends, Ed &
Maryjane Savacool

250

Hopewell Rocks, Bay of Fundy, Canada

Lunch with Savacools in Nova Scotia

B&B at Antigonish, Nova Scotia (haunted house)

Cozy sitting room in the haunted house

Vacation car to Prince Edward Island

Joshua Outlook B&B, Hunters Point, PEI

Bob Lutz and me at PEI

Willy Krauch, owner of smoked salmon store

Condo at
Kennebunkport, Maine

President H. W. Bush

Mrs. Barbara Bush

253

General Director of FIM

FIM Retirement luncheon
with Board of Directors

My retirement cake

254

# Milestones

On June 4, 2005 was a milestone in Elaine and my lives. It was our 50th wedding anniversary. Our kids had talked about this special day previously and wondered what we were going to do as a celebration. We both told our kids that all we would want was to have a nice dinner together as a family.

Rick, Roxann and their families worked very hard to make our day a special day. We were invited to come to Silver Creek Country Club where our son-in-law, Jim, is a member and have our anniversary dinner there. The kids insisted that someone would come to pick us up at the designated time. On the designated day, to our surprise the doorbell rang and a chauffeur escorted us out to the limousine. He opened the back door for Elaine and then came around to the other side to open the door for me. Wow, what service! This was really living. As I sat in the back of this spacious and luxurious vehicle, I cupped my hand together and shouted to the driver: "Take the long way." I sat there looking at all the switches and knobs and began to test them out to see what would happen.

As we drove to the country club we sat close together holding hands and just enjoying the ride. Soon we arrived at the country club. Roxann, Jim, Rick and Tracy met us as we pulled up to the entrance door. They escorted us into the lobby. The stair railings were lined with beautiful flowers and chiffon material. The doors were opened and we saw a sea of friendly faces congratulating us with a shout of "Surprise!" There was a gentleman at the piano playing music softly. I don't know how the kids did it but they had contacted many of our old friends that were no longer living in our area.

Jim served as the MC and did a great job. Rev. Leon Overpeck had us come forward under an arbor covered with beautiful flowers to renew our vows. We met Leon at Berean Bible School in 1954 when Elaine and I were students there. We have remained close friends ever since. After the vows were renewed I could kiss the bride. The meal was out of this world and all the invited guests couldn't say enough about the beauty of the room and the service. It was an excitingly wonderful day, and one we will enjoy and remember. We are very proud of our kids and their mates and all their extra effort they did to make our 50th the best day of our lives.

I remained involved with FIM as General Director Emeritus. In my new capacity I set up a regular schedule to meet with Pastor Fellowship groups in Pennsylvania, New Jersey and New York. This gave me opportunity to regularly represent the ministry of FIM and also for speaking opportunities in some of those churches represented in the fellowship group. I continued to accept speaking opportunities in churches mainly as a guest speaker or pulpit supply. I also was asked to sit in on the FIM board meetings and contribute as needed. I continued in this position until 2008 when I had completed 50 years of ministry.

A surprise retirement service was secretly arranged by Elaine and Pastor Dave Klase, senior pastor of Exeter Bible Church on my behalf. Pastor Klase asked me to come to the church on December 2nd and be prepared to give a ten-minute overview of my fifty years of ministry. Elaine had invited a large group of our friends and family members to attend the service. It was a snowy, icy day. I found out later that because of the weather a group of people from First Baptist Church in Phillipsburg including Bob & Lois Allshouse, were planning on being in attendance but because of the bad roads were not able to make the trip. Bob was to be the guest organist as a surprise for me. All of my family was present and others who braved the weather. Karen Smith was the surprise vocalist. Karen had been my secretary for many years and is a very talented soloist. It was a very uplifting day for me.

The next several months I was asked to speak at Whitehall Bible Fellowship Church. They were without a pastor for about a year and a half and other Bible Fellowship retired pastors were speaking on a rotating schedule. One of the pastors was unavailable for one of those Sundays and I took his place on the schedule. In April, I was asked by Mark Nielson, chairman of the Elder Board if I could give them any more time to speak. I consented to be their interim pastor and began my ministry with them on May 25, 2008. I served as interim until they called a pastor. He began his ministry with the church on August 2, 2009.

Elaine and I decided not to continue attending Whitehall BFC but would allow some time to pass for the new pastor to become familiar with the people and the vision of the church.

Several months had passed since the new pastor came to Whitehall BFC when we were invited to return and teach a Sunday school class. We began teaching the class October 25, 2009. A short time later I was asked to serve as visitation pastor. I taught the Adult Sunday school class and did the visitation ministry until the end of October 2013. At that time Northern Valley Evangelical Free Church was without a pastor and the interim pastor that was with them submitted his resignation to become effective September 1, 2013. One of the elders from Northern Valley called me to ask if I would consider meeting with the elders to discuss the possibility of me becoming their interim while they considered the next step in seeking a pastor. The congregation was small and could not afford to hire a full-time pastor. I met with the elders and agreed to be their interim pastor.

I met with the pastor of Whitehall BFC and told him of the invitation to be the interim pastor at Northern Valley. I submitted my resignation to be effective November 1, 2013. I was thanked by the pastor for the time I had given to Whitehall BFC.

I became the interim pastor of Northern Valley Evangelical Free Church in New Tripoli, PA starting with November 3, 2013. While serving Northern Valley I failed a stress test and underwent a heart valve replacement on March 21, 2014. During the surgery an aneurysm was discovered behind my heart. What should have taken about two hours of surgical procedure turned out to be almost nine hours. I lost a considerable amount of blood because the surgical team could not stop the bleeding. After doing a reverse procedure the bleeding stopped and I was sent to the Intensive Care Unit. I progressed daily and after one week I returned home to prepare for physical therapy. I slowly gained back some of my strength and returned to the pulpit on May 4th. The following months were difficult because my strength was returning much slower than I anticipated. I was unable to continue ministering as interim pastor and found it necessary to resign effective November 1, 2014.

We were nearing another milestone in our lives. June 4th, 2015 would be our 60th wedding anniversary. Once again our kids wanted to know what we had planned to do to celebrate this event. Again, all we wanted was to have dinner together with our family. We were invited to come to Roxann and Jim's house for a cookout. But unbeknown to us it was another surprise with many of our friends waiting for us. We didn't expect anything because when we pulled into their home we didn't see any other cars than those of our family members. The kids had the surprise guests drive their cars and park them behind the trees in the grassy area behind the house. For entertainment they invited a barber shop quartet to sing some of the old favorite quartet songs. It was another unforgettable day.

## 50th Wedding Anniversary

1955     2005

A lifetime of loving, caring and sharing . . .
Please join the children and grandchildren
as we celebrate the Fiftieth Wedding Anniversary
of Dick and Elaine Ruth
at a surprise reception
on Sunday, the fifth of June
two thousand and five
at four o'clock in the afternoon
Silver Creek Country Club
900 Linden Street
Hellertown, Pennsylvania

Your friendship to our parents and grandparents is a gift,
no more is needed.

Son-in-law, Jim Wagner as MC

Renewing our wedding vows with Rev. Leon Overpeck

50 years of
ministry, with
FIM board
members and
their wives

50 years of ministry,
with family

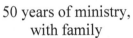

Whitehall BFC

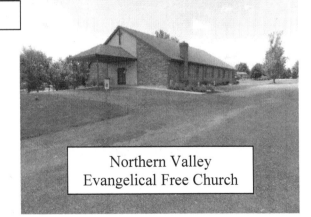

Northern Valley
Evangelical Free Church

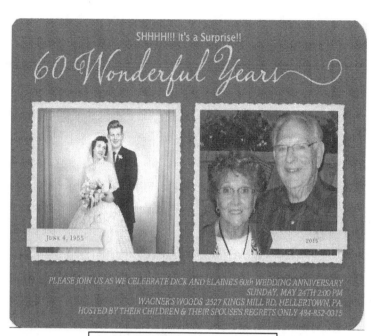

60th Wedding Anniversary

# Looking Back and Looking Forward

For the past several years I have mentored several younger pastors on a regular basis. I am continuing to do mentoring ministry and have added two missionary couples with whom we are in contact via e-mail or telephone. These mentoring sessions keep me busy and in contact with their individual ministries, etc.

Over the years we have enjoyed traveling to Nova Scotia, Prince Edward Island, three times to Bermuda, once to the Holy Lands and numerous trips to Kennebunkport, Maine, several trips to Florida to visit Elaine's family and our friends who moved there from our church in Phillipsburg, NJ. We also attended many National Conventions of IFCA International that were held every June in different parts of the country. In our younger years, we enjoyed traveling when we could and were also very thankful we had the opportunities.

I have also enjoyed hunting, fishing and playing golf. Rick and I continue to hunt deer in the Poconos and in our specially built deer hut at Roxann and Jim's home in Hellertown.

Throughout our married life, Elaine and I have had the pleasure and privilege of entertaining many friends in our home and have also been entertained on many occasions.

Some other short trips come to mind as I complete my life's story. On two separate occasions we spent a weekend at Cape May, NJ with Nancy and Neil Taylor. We always enjoyed ourselves even if it rained both weekends while we were there.

Doris and Joe Wire invited us to join them for a week at their friend's home two blocks from the beach in Ocean City, NJ. We enjoyed early morning walks on the board walk and delicious seafood dinners together. We always enjoyed taking many day trips to our favorite places or trying to find new adventures on our own or with friends.

The Lord has blessed us with a wonderful family who have made us proud as they have done well in their respective vocations. Roxann is a Professor, teaching in the department of nursing at Cedar Crest College and her husband Jim has his own environmental consulting business. Rick is doing well in the corporate business field as Sales Manager for Mars Inc., and his wife Tracy is a receptionist for an optometrist. We have four grandchildren each busy with their individual careers and two great-grandchildren.

In summary, as I look back over almost 60 years since I preached my first sermon, I still cannot imagine what my life would have been if I hadn't accepted the Lord as my Saviour as a young boy, or dedicated my life to Him as a teenager. There have been more joys than sorrows, more answers to prayer than disappointments and the deep settled peace to know I was doing what the Lord had called me to do. Many portions of Scripture have affected my thinking and my life but I will list only two.

Isaiah 26:3-4 *"You will keep him in perfect peace, whose mind is stayed on You, because he trusts in You. Trust in the Lord forever, for in the Lord is everlasting strength."*

I Corinthians 4:2 *"Moreover it is required in stewards that one be found faithful."*

Early in my ministry an older saint in the Lord gave me this advice and I have applied it to my life as well as passed it on to many others. It simply is this: "Knees down in prayer. Chin up in determination."

On this day of April 26th, 2017, I have completed the task I set out to do. It has been time well spent as I enjoyed reminiscing over these past 80 years.

My life has been a series of adventures. Some were disappointing, grievous and heart breaking while all the others were joyous, exciting and very rewarding. Being raised in a poor family helped me to appreciate the many blessings the Lord so graciously has given to me and my family.

There are many hymns, songs and choruses that have thrilled my soul and ministered to me at just the right time. However the one that thrilled me and ministered to me the most, brings tears to my eyes every time I hear it sung, is: "Until Then," by Ray Price.

> *My heart can sing when I pause to remember.*
> *A heartache here is but a stepping stone.*
> *Along a path that's wondering always upward,*
> *This troubled world is not my final home.*
> *But until then my heart will go on singing,*
> *Until then with joy I'll carry on.*
> *Until the day my eyes behold my Saviour*
> *Until the day God calls me home.*

I don't know what a day will bring but I know that whatever it is, the Lord will direct my steps and provide for my every need as He so faithfully has done over all these years. I face each day with the promise of the Lord that He will never leave me or forsake me. Someday at God's timing, I will have the privilege of seeing Christ face to face and be in His presence forever in heaven.

Some of my adventures

Some fun pictures

Elaine and me with our
children, Roxann and Rick

Roxann and Jim;
Rick and Tracy

268

My grandchildren:
Laurile, Alexis, Jake and
Terry

My grandchildren: Laurile
and Alexis

My granddaughter, Laurile with her husband Jamey, and my two great-grandchildren, Logan and Amelia

Made in the USA
Middletown, DE
08 April 2018